NOAH WEBSTER

(Courtesy of G. & C. Merriam Co., Publishers of the Merriam-Webster Dictionaries.)

NOAH
WEBSTER

John S. Morgan

MASON/CHARTER

NEW YORK 1975

First Edition

Library of Congress Cataloging in Publication Data

Morgan, John Smith, 1921-
   Noah Webster.

   Bibliography: p.
   1. Webster, Noah, 1758-1843.
PE64.W5M67   423'.092'4 [B]   75-5883
ISBN 0-88405-108-0

CONTENTS

ACKNOWLEDGMENTS

The Noah Webster Foundation, West Hartford, Conn., preserves Webster's birthplace and is a storehouse of memorabilia concerning him, his family, and his times. Among the many people who helped in the preparation of this biography with facts, suggestions, and advice, the following gave notable aid:

Homer D. Babbidge, Jr., Master of Timothy Dwight College, Yale University, New Haven, Connecticut.

Mrs. Howard B. Field, great-granddaughter of Noah Webster and granddaughter of Harriet Webster Cobb Fowler, Durham, Connecticut.

Crawford Lincoln, Vice President and Secretary, G. & C. Merriam Company, Springfield, Massachusetts.

Dr. Freeman W. Meyer, Professor of History, University of Connecticut, Storrs, Connecticut.

PART ONE

Webster, the Man and His World

Chapter 1

FOR GOD, FOR COUNTRY

In March 1765 a six-year-old boy named Noah Webster may have seen, for the first time, the full alphabet printed in capital and small letters and in Roman and italic styles. *The Connecticut Courant,* published in Hartford by the printers and booksellers Hudson & Goodwin, had devoted nearly half of its front page to the alphabet, so readers could show their children the varieties of the letters. It is likely that the boy's father, Noah Webster, Sr., subscribed to the paper, because he was a literate and progressive man, a leader in his community of West Hartford; and if he received the paper, he surely showed it to his children, especially to young Noah, who must have already displayed signs of precociousness. Yet one can only speculate. Noah Webster, Jr., who was to write so prodigious a volume, the 70,000-word dictionary of 1828, always showed reticence about his private life and feelings. In fact, little is known concerning his youth until he reached the age of 14. The speculation has validity, however. The *Courant* carried young Webster's first article, published in 1780, and Hudson & Goodwin printed his first book, a speller. The personal and business connections that Webster maintained all his life with the *Courant* and with its publisher may indeed have started when he saw, as a boy, the elements of the language to which he devoted his life printed on the front page of the newspaper.

Young Noah was born on October 16, 1758, in a house that still stands at 227 South Main Street in West Hartford, Connecticut. He was born in the parlor chamber, so-called because it was directly above the parlor in the northern half of the house, the original half, to which the southern part, constructed elsewhere, had been added later. The practice of adding sections to a house as a family grew was a common one in the early eighteenth century, when the house was built by Noah Webster's grandfather. At the time of Noah's birth, the structure consisted of just four rooms built around a central chimney and fireplaces. This was known as the Connecticut floor plan. At that time the house was white. Not until Noah, Jr., had moved away was a lean-to added, containing a new kitchen, bedroom, and pantry. Nor was it painted the New England barn red until the young man had left its confines. A back 'L' was not built until the nineteenth century when the house had passed into the hands of another family.

The home stands on a ridge. In the boy's day, the small flat doorstep at the front commanded a fine view eastward toward Hartford. At the back, the westward view was, and still is, of the pleasant Farmington hills. In young Noah's boyhood and youth, West Hartford was an industrious and thrifty farming community of scattered houses, pastures, meadows, and stone walls. Although not wealthy, it remained moderately prosperous in this period, never needing a poorhouse.

Butter, cheese, and wool were among the chief products of the farms in the area. Boys as young as 12 were already plowing. Joel Barlow, who was Noah's Yale classmate and who shared a similar farming boyhood in nearby Redding, wrote:

> From morn to noon, from noon to night,
> I daily drove the plow,
> And foddered like an honest wight,
> Sheep, oxen, horse, and cow.

He could have added that he also hoed and picked corn, dug potatoes, cut hay, milked the cows, and helped his father and brothers at slaughtering time.

Even a farm as small as the 80-acre Webster holdings had to be nearly self-sufficient. About the only outside services came from the sawmill, a shoe shop, a wagon shop, the blacksmith, the miller, and the general storekeeper. Yet the narrow New England farm life offered some social life. The Sunday visit to the village meeting-house provided social contacts as well as seemingly endless sermons. The boys could see the girls they had perhaps kissed furtively among the corn rows during the week while gathering roasting ears. In October, both youths and maidens gathered for cornhusking bees, which Noah would later adapt for spelling bees. Under the light of whale-oil lamps, "brown, corn-fed nymphs and strong, hard-handed beaux" sat in circles about the grain to shuck corn and play post office. They husked energetically until someone found a red ear. The lucky boy could then kiss all the girls; the lucky girl would walk blushingly around the circle to choose her particular boy. The girl who husked a bad ear, however, could hit the nearest boy over the head with it.

No games or frivolities were allowed from sundown on Saturday and all day Sunday. While sports were not unknown, no evidence exists that young Noah participated much. Certainly in later life he rarely indulged in frivolities. He enjoyed eating, however. As a youth he may well have acquired his taste for chicken, pudding, blackberry pies, and sweets of all kinds. Maple trees dotted nearly every Connecticut farm, producing sap for the maple sugar that had become a staple in the colony. In those days a great treat was candy (then meaning broken pieces of maple sugar) for dessert. Many a Connecticut farm also boasted a tub of sweetening, a wooden sugar bucket containing thick maple syrup.

So, although life was arduous during Noah Webster's boyhood, it wasn't all work, and while living conditions were spare by today's standards, with the Webster family of seven crowded into four rooms, the boy was fortunate enough to grow up in a healthy, attractive, and quiet community.

Young Noah lived in the house of his birth until he entered Yale in 1774. This was the last time he dwelt permanently in the old Webster house, although he returned temporarily during vacations and a few times after graduation. No evidence exists that Noah, Jr., was particularly unhappy at home; yet his driving ambition and restless energy kept him on the move most of his life. Although he didn't know then, nor did he know for several decades, precisely what he wanted to do, he did know that he wouldn't farm his father's acres. His father was in what was then called the middling class of the era; nevertheless, Noah, Jr., wanted a different life, a life that was more along professional rather than agricultural lines.

Noah, Jr., showed an academic bent early in his life, and his father frequently found the boy lying in the shade reading when he was supposed to be working in the fields. Young Noah showed such promise and pertinacity that he got more education than any of his four brothers and sisters, despite the fact that he was not the eldest son. In those days, an ambitious but not wealthy father usually arranged for his eldest son to receive the best education when he could not afford to educate all his children. Abraham (or Abram) was the first son in the family, born in 1751. The eldest child, born in 1749, was the girl Mercy. Another sister, Jerusha, was born after Abraham in 1756. Fourth in order was Noah, then another brother, Charles, born in 1762. The girls married young and did not figure prominently in their famous brother's life. Noah perhaps felt beholden to them for the educational advantages granted him, because he later helped his brothers and sisters educate their children, especially the two sons of Charles.

Until a child reached the age of 14, very narrow bounds confined his secular studies. A Connecticut law required that elementary schools be conducted each year under the control of the church societies. In West Hartford, the Ecclesiastical Society of the local Congregational Church operated the school and controlled many other matters of public interest. In fact, it exercised all the functions of government for the community. A committee of three members administered secular affairs, but devoted so much time to education that it became known as the school committee. The society had the power to tax in order to support the school, the church, and other community functions. Church and schoolhouse were built side by side, emphasizing the close connection between the two. The society ran the West Hartford school from 1711 until 1795.

Although West Hartford's elementary school operated for 11 months each year, children didn't attend that long. Youngsters of four to six or seven years of age went during the summer, taught usually by one of the mothers in the community. Because of the chores during the spring, summer, and autumn months, older children attended during the winter, taught by a schoolmaster if the school had one. If the school did not have one, and often it did not, then the better educated citizens tried to substitute, or perhaps one of the more advanced and older pupils filled in. The communities of colonial America frequently held neither schoolmasters nor teaching in high esteem. Many teachers followed Goldsmith's words:

> Let schoolmasters puzzle their brains
> With grammar and nonsense and learning,
> Good liquor I stoutly maintain,
> Gives genius a better discerning.

Meager salaries, the practice of having to board around among the parish families, and wretched schoolhouses and other facilities did not attract many high-grade people to the profession. Schoolhouse roofs leaked and thin walls let in the cold. The equipment itself was even worse than the buildings. Tables designed for the younger children cramped the taller ones. In 1781 Webster described school conditions thus: "When I was a schoolboy, the greatest part of the scholars did not employ more than an hour in a day, either in writing or in reading; while five hours of the school time was spent in idleness, in cutting the tables and benches to pieces, in carrying on pin lotteries, or perhaps in some more roguish tricks."

Because children did destroy property and waste time, few schools had maps, globes, or even many books. By 1765 New England schools had universally adopted Thomas Dilworth's *New Guide to the English Tongue*, containing a series of spelling and reading lessons and a short grammar. The reading lessons dealt mostly with religious subjects. A Psalter or Bible was the only other book in young Noah's first school. The teacher used this to test skill in reading, with emphasis on volume and enunciation, not on understanding.

Young Noah's first school had neither slates nor pencils. He recorded the master's dictation with goose-quill pens, ink, and paper. He continued to use quill pens all his life, long after they were obsolete. He probably had to make his own ink for school from mashed and boiled walnut or butternut hulls, with vinegar and salt added. This resulted in a brown ink. To get black, he could have added soot. Because blue required more expensive materials and a more complex recipe, he probably never used that color.

Despite the bad conditions, the desire for more learning somehow infected young Noah. He showed at an early age an understanding and interest in words not usually found among children, and he displayed a decided love for the few books he had. When he was 14, he asked his father to let him study the classics with the Reverend Nathan Perkins, who had just become the minister for the West Hartford Congregational Parish. Noah, Sr., hesitated because of the expense and because of the fact that the boy wasn't the eldest. But young Noah persisted and insisted, and finally began his studies in 1772.

When Perkins began his ministry in West Hartford, he was a young man just out of Princeton; already, he must have been a gifted teacher and an inspiring human being. He held his ministry until his death 56 years later. During that time, he prepared more than 150 young men for college, and also instructed some 30 candidates for the ministry.

Noah didn't return to Perkins the next winter probably for economic reasons, but went to the Hopkins Grammar School in Hartford instead. Although Hopkins was a fairly respectable primary school, young Noah found that its instruction didn't measure up to Perkins's standards. So he used his persuasive skills again on his father, who finally allowed him to return to Perkins's tutelage to finish his preparatory education.

Such formal study comprised only part of his education, however. Noah Webster came from a deeply religious family whose members practiced the Congregationalism dominant in that time and place. Noah, Sr., a deacon in the church, carefully educated his children in religious principles. Young Noah may have rebelled somewhat at the austerity of this brand of Calvinism, because he later confessed: "Being educated in a religious family under pious parents, I had in early life some religious impressions, but being too young to understand fully the doctrines of the Christian religion . . . I lost those impressions. . . ." It is difficult to imagine such impressions fading. The religious instruction at school, the Sunday services lasting two to three hours, grace at every meal, daily Bible readings, and frequent visits from the parish minister all formed so much a part of his early life that he couldn't possibly have lost their impressions, and probably carried them with him all his life.

Young Noah received his education, too, through his physical labors, for although he attended school between the ages of 14 and 16, he also spent at least half his waking hours working on his father's farm. By the time he was 16, he could have made his living as a farmer. Indeed, as an adult, he supplemented his income for ten years with his agricultural activities in Amherst, Massachusetts. He wrote frequently and knowledgeably on farming subjects and experiments he had performed. Many of his other writings are filled with rural references.

Thus, in common with many Connecticut boys of the late eighteenth century, Noah, Jr., grew up in an atmosphere compounded of hard work and a particularly austere brand of Congregationalist piety. This bred in him habits of industry, frugality, and rectitude, but, somewhat negatively, it instilled in him a rather pompous disposition as well.

Young Noah had yet another important educational advantage —the yeasty times in which he lived. His life began amid the commotions and hardships of the French and Indian War, in which his father had soldiered and had reached the rank of lieutenant. The year of his birth was the time of the disastrous repulse of Abercromby in his attack on Ticonderoga, in which he lost 2,000 men —a frightful casualty list, especially for those days. The war was over in the American colonies by 1761, so that among the boy's earliest recollections must have been mingled the talk that went on in his father's house about the incidents of this bloody struggle. Noah, Sr., was a man of vigorous intellect who had a lively interest in current events, despite his limited education. He was for many years a justice of the peace in the town of Hartford and a captain in the local militia, in addition to holding an office in the church.

In Connecticut, government was part of everyday life, and the Webster family was more inextricably connected with it than most through the elder Noah's judicial, military, and religious posts. Nevertheless, in those days when a person had to be multitalented to make a living, it was not particularly uncommon for one man to hold so many disparate positions.

An interest in government could also have come to young Noah by inheritance. He was a direct descendent on both sides of his family from two Colonial governors. On the paternal side, he was the great, great, great grandson of John Webster, chosen governor of Connecticut Colony in 1656, a post he held until 1659 when he moved to Massachusetts. John's eldest son, Robert, probably born in England, returned to Hartford after his father moved to Massachusetts, and became a selectman there. His son, John, lived until 1695, leaving seven children. His youngest son, Daniel, young Noah's grandfather, was born in 1693.

Noah Webster is often confused with Daniel Webster, who was a contemporary, friend, and Massachusetts legislator. Yet no blood relationship has been discovered. The name *Webster* means "female weaver," and families which bear this occupational name are not necessarily related. Despite his friendship with the legislator Webster, Noah in later life often grew irritated at the confusion compounded by the fact that his own grandfather bore the same first name.

On his maternal side, Noah, Jr., was the great, great grandson of William Bradford, governor of the Plymouth Colony from 1621 until his death in 1651. Young Noah's mother, Mercy Steele Webster, was "gentle, loving . . . looking well to the ways of her household." Although his mother was a woman of intelligence and energy, his father appears to have had the more dominant personality. Noah, Sr., had the greater longevity of the two as well, living for 91 years until 1813, while his wife died in 1794 at the age of 67.

From his parents, young Noah inherited a jutting jaw, bushy and reddish hair, a ruddy complexion, brown eyes, a lithe body, and a quick and springy step. He talked a great deal and occasionally lost control of his temper, a traditional characteristic of redheads. These qualities probably got him into trouble at home from time to time, because the doctrine that a child "should be seen but not heard" was no empty motto in eighteenth-century Calvinist Connecticut. A child's silence and submission to his elders were taken for granted. One can picture young Noah enduring a Sunday rigid in a ladderback chair while elder brother Abraham played the flute and the family sang Watt's Psalms or while the deacon read the Bible.

That is how Connecticut's reputation for steady habits arose. Yet young Noah endured it. When he was 38 years old, after time had perhaps glossed over the worst of his memories, he could even laud the steady habits which "are formed by a singular machinery in the body politic, which takes the child as soon as he can speak, checks his natural independence and passions, makes him subordinate to superior age, to the laws of the state, to town and parochial institutions—initiates him in the business of government by making him an active party in local regulations, and in short molding him into a peaceable citizen, an intelligent man, and an independent, but rational freeman."

Thomas Jefferson once described the people of New England thus: "They are cool, sober, laborious, persevering, independent, jealous of their liberties and those of others, interested, chicaning, superstitious and hypocritical in their religion." Except for the qualities of chicanery and superstition, the characteristics apply to young Noah, for he was a boy of New England and especially of Connecticut. In later life, in a rare burst of emotion, he wrote: "New England is certainly a phenomenon in civil and political establishments, and in my opinion not only young gentlemen from our sister states, but from every quarter of the globe would do well to pass a few years of their life among us, and acquire our habits of thinking and living."

In the late eighteenth century, Connecticut was one of the most prosperous and stable of the original thirteen colonies. Farming was the economic backbone. In 1680 the colony supported only about 12,500 people. Less than a century later, in 1774, it supported 198,000, one of the most densely settled of all American colonies. Foreign travelers expressed surprise that it appeared as closely populated as England. They passed continually through towns and villages. In 1774 Connecticut's thickly populated area ran along the coast, with tongues spreading northward from Stratford up the Housatonic and Naugatuck rivers to Waterbury, from New Haven northeast to the Connecticut River Valley at Middletown and thence upriver to the Massachusetts line, and from New London northward up the Thames River to Norwich.

Congregationalism dominated as the religious, social, and political force, but dissenting churches enjoyed tolerance so long as they did not threaten Congregationalism's political domination.

During the century before the American Revolution, Connecticut enjoyed more self-government than any other mainland British colony except Rhode Island. At the local level the towns were authorized by the colonial government to make all necessary "orders, rules, and constitutions." Thus, they conducted their affairs almost without check, as the voters annually elected a host of officials such as selectmen, treasurers, listers, constables, packers of

meat, sealers of dry measures and weights, fence viewers, horse
branders, pound and key keepers, tithing men, and grand jurors,
as well as two deputies to the assembly's house of representatives.
The colonial government acted almost like an independent republic
by keeping contacts with royal authority to a minimum.

Colonial Connecticut was never a democracy because its religious leaders opposed such a system. Nurtured on the Calvinistic
concept of man as being inherently evil, they abhorred rule by the
masses and advocated rule by the elect. Rigorous religious and
property requirements were established for the right to vote. They
required that before a man could vote in a town or county election
he must be an inhabitant of legal age, a householder, a man "of
sober conversation," and a possessor of a freehold estate. In addition, he had to take the freemen's oath before an assistant or justice
of the peace and get a certificate from the town selectmen attesting
"quiet and peaceable behavior and civil conversation." In 1766 less
than half the adult population of Connecticut qualified as freemen.
These arrangements, nevertheless, gave Connecticut remarkable
political stability until about 1765. That year saw the climax of a
depression which followed the French and Indian War. In addition,
Great Britain chose that time to pass the ill-advised Stamp Act as
a means of getting the colonists to help pay for the war.

These events were certainly discussed in the Webster
household, because Noah, Sr., was a freeman and an ardent sup-
porter of the established order. If only by osmosis, young Noah
early absorbed an interest in, knowledge of, and instinct for public
affairs that fostered the patriotism which motivated his later life.

Nearly every French traveler commented on the high wage
rates encountered in New England and New York. Pay for laborers
and servants was higher there than in Europe. The day after a ship
loaded with Scotsmen landed in New York, "there was not one
who was not hired out and busy." The restless mobility of the
population also astounded foreign visitors. "Four times running,"
wrote Mederic Louis Moreau de Saint-Mery, the French historian
(1750–1819) who lived in exile in Philadelphia during the 1790s,
"they will break land for a new home, abandoning without a
thought the house in which they were born, the church where they
learned about God, the tombs of their fathers, the friends of their
childhood, the companions of their youth, and all the pleasures of
their first society."

Americans achieved their remarkable mobility despite bad roads and uncomfortable vehicles. A system of allowing people to work off their taxes by clearing and repairing a section of the roads was common. This meant that the roads would be decidedly uneven in quality. Boulders, stumps, and mudholes were commonly encountered in the country roads. A coach driver always carried an ax to clear obstructions, and his male passengers were called upon to push when necessary.

A common passenger vehicle of wholly American origin was the pleasure wagon. There was little pleasure in it, however, even though it was designed to haul people, not freight. The body had no springs, although the seat bounced on two hickory cantilevers that were intended to make the ride more bearable. This vehicle was the ancestor of the buggy.

In cities with better roads, the carriage or "wonderful one-hoss shay" appeared. South of Boston it was called a chair or more often a *cheer*. It boasted hickory springs from which the back of the body was suspended, and it usually had no top; if it did, the top was an immovable one made of canvas.

The wealthy imported sedan chairs. Massachusetts Governor John Winthrop had one as early as 1646; Ben Franklin still used one in 1789, although it was an anachronism by then. However, its various names survived, and chair, *cheer,* or *shay* (a corruption of the French chaise) remained in use as the names for a primitive carriage.

New Englanders spoke through their noses with a nasal twang and drawl. Benjamin Franklin remarked that "the Boston manner, turn of phrase, and even tone of voice and accent in pronunciation all please, and seem to revive and refresh me." But Nicholas Cresswell, an English traveler, wrote that the New Englanders "have a sort of whining cadence which I cannot describe."

New Englanders said *dew* for do, *tew* for too, *keow* for cow, *datter* for daughter, *sass* for sauce, *sarve* for serve, *desarve* for deserve, *consate* for conceit, *desate* for deceit, *obleege* for oblige and *deef* for deaf. They flattened the final *a* in America, or at least the poet did who composed this welcome to General Washington:

> Hail, bright auspicious day!
> Long shall America
> Thy praise resound.

The New England selection of syllables for stressing also proved distinctive, as for example: *admírable, dispútable, compárable.* Noah Webster later defended most New England usages, but he did attack as improper such pronunciations as *advarsity* for adversity, *apurn* for apron, *backard* for backward, *chimbly* for chimney, *kiver* for cover, *gal* for girl, and the almost universal dropping of the final "g" in such words as going and coming.

During the Revolutionary War, a New England infantryman composed a "Song of the Minute Men" and spelled it phonetically:

Now tew oure Station Let us march and randevouse with
   pleasure.
We have bee like Brave minut men to sarve so Great a
   Treasure.
We let them se amediately that we are men of mettle.
We boys here that fere no nois will never flinch for Battle.

New Englanders had more than an accent; they also had a manner of speaking. Instead of saying *you must,* they more commonly asked, *is it not best?* They gave opinions with an indecisive tone: *you had better, I believe.*

French travelers in New England, even those who spoke English, found that they had to acquire a new, colorful, and native-born vocabulary: backwoods, backcountry, catboat, pungy, bullfrog, eggplant, lightning bug, razorback. They struggled with proper names: the town of Norege in Connecticut, those well-known Indian tribes, Scherokys and Tchactas. In Newburyport, a Frenchman found himself worsted after the polite visit of a colonel "whose name was pronounced something like Wigsleps." (Non-New Englanders also expressed bafflement when first confronted with the Massachusetts family of Wigglesworth.)

This was the stuff with which young Noah would eventually make a career. This was the material he would use to fashion a uniform language that would help weld a new nation together. But he didn't know this at the age of 16. Indeed, it would take him decades to grope toward the obscure and unlikely profession of lexicography.

As he went off to Yale, he was an outwardly bumptious and self-assured boy, but inwardly he was uncertain. All he knew was that he had the support of his parents for whatever he chose to do. His father wrote him: "I rejoice to hear that there is a prospect of your doing good and benefiting yourself. I wish to have you serve your generation and do good in the world and be useful and may so behave as to gain the esteem of all virtuous people that are acquainted with you and gain a comfortable subsistence . . ."

Chapter 2

AND FOR YALE

Noah Webster, Sr., grew so interested in his second son's career that he mortgaged the farm to pay the boy's college expenses at Yale. More than once the father rode the 50 miles to New Haven on horseback in order to bring his boy home; once he even walked back and let his son ride, saying that he was better able to walk.

Knowingly or unknowingly, the elder Webster had introduced his son into a hotbed of revolutionary fervor. The radicalism of some of the students and faculty at Yale in the late 1960s and early 1970s may not seem such a surprising phenomenon if viewed in the context of events 200 years earlier. Loyalist Thomas Jones characterized his alma mater as early as 1750 as a "nursery of sedition, of faction, and republicanism." The class of 1769 appeared at graduation dressed entirely in the manufactures of their own country.

At the commencement of 1770, three months after the Boston Massacre but still five years before Lexington, John Trumbull composed these lines:

> For pleasing arts behold her matchless charms.
> The first in letters, as the first in arms,
> See bolder genius quit the narrow shore,
> And realms of science, yet untraced, explore,
> Hiding in brightness of superior day,
> The fainting gleam of Europe's setting ray.

In 1771 John Trumbull, age 21, and Timothy Dwight, age 19, became tutors, each in charge of a class at Yale. Both were ardent spokesmen for the new transcendent loyalty and vision of a greater America.

Trumbull preached nationalism in prose, too:

The heroic love of Liberty, the manly fortitude, the generosity of sentiment, for which we have been so justly celebrated, seem to promise the future advancement and established duration of our glory. Happy . . . have been our late struggles for liberty! They have awakened the spirit of freedom; they have rectified the manners of the times; recalled to our minds the glorious independence of former ages, fired us with the views of fame, and by filling our thoughts with contempt of the imported articles of luxury, have raised an opposition, not only to the illegal power, but to the effeminate manners of Britain.

Although ineffective as a leader of Yale, President Naphtali Daggett, who had served pro tempore since October 1766, regularly preached independence in his sermons and elsewhere:

When I considered the controversy to be truly and simply this, whether this large and fertile country, settled with infinite toil and dangers by our fathers, should be our own free possession or at the disposal of a bankrupt prodigal state in Europe, I could not hesitate a moment, and I cannot but view it in its probable, or rather certain, consequence the most important contest that hath taken place on the globe for many centuries past. . . . Under this view of the justice and high importance of the controversy, I feel willing to risque my temporal all in support of it.

He was to do just that when, in July 1779, the British invaded New Haven. Hastily gathered volunteers, including Yale students, vainly contested their advance. But the British were distracted by a solitary sniper on their flank. The septuagenarian Daggett was firing at them with a fowling piece as antiquated as he. The redcoats captured him, beat him, removed his shoes and forced him to march five miles to New Haven. He died soon after from the wounds and injuries sustained in that adventure.

Beginning in 1774, young Noah Webster absorbed an exciting concept of American nationality and destiny—the concept of a nation—primarily from Trumbull and Dwight. The latter had become an outspoken advocate for independence by July 1775, a full year before the signing of the Declaration of Independence.

Webster's class of 1778 had as its tutor Joseph Buckminster, but the class ahead of his had Dwight. Despite the fact that Timothy Dwight was responsible for another class, Noah's classmates flocked around him, attracted by his patriotism, his derisive criticism of superiors, and his ability to instill in the students a sense of their high personal and social responsibilities.

Among Dwight's little-known contributions to the cause of American nationhood was the composition of the words and music to *Columbia,* America's quasi-official national anthem until *The Star Spangled Banner*, which contains these lines:

> Columbia, Columbia, to glory rise,
> The Queen of the World and child of the skies!
> Thy Genius commands thee; with rapture behold,
> While ages on ages thy splendors unfold,
> Thy reign is the last and the noblest of time.
> Most fruitful thy soil, most inviting thy clime;
> Let the crimes of the east ne'er encrimson thy name,
> Be freedom, and science, and virtue thy fame.

Dwight even inspired the prosaic Webster to write poetry. Webster praises him thus as a teacher and poet:

> Hail, rising genius, whose celestial fire
> Warms the glad soul to tune the sacred lyre;
> Glow in your breast; you reach a fostering hand
> To nourish science and adorn the land.

In 1776, shortly after the Declaration of Independence had been published in New Haven, Dwight pronounced the valedictory address to the seniors, calling in heroic terms for exceptional qualities from the class:

You should by no means consider yourselves as members of a small neighborhood, town or colony only, but as being concerned in laying the foundations of American greatness. Your wishes, your designs, your labors, are not to be confined by the narrow bounds of the present age, but are to comprehend succeeding generations, and be pointed to immortality.

You are to act, not like inhabitants of a village, nor like beings of an hour, but like citizens of a world, and like candidates for a name that shall survive the conflagration. These views will enlarge your minds, expand the grasp of your benevolences, ennoble all your conduct, and crown you with wreaths which cannot fade. . . . Remember that you are to act for the empire of America, and for a long succession of ages.

Such exhortations remained with Noah, Jr., for the rest of his life. They inspired others, too. Nathan Hale, who was three years older than Webster, also came under the influence of Trumbull and Dwight while at Yale; he later regretted that he had but one life to give to his country when he was hanged by the British in 1776 for spying.

No wonder that by 1774 the zeal for independence at the New Haven college had reached a height perhaps exceeded only in Boston. All the students at Yale avidly followed the events of that year. The British prime minister, Lord North, who felt that he had had enough trouble with Boston, decided to punish the town with a demonstration of authority. He drafted the Boston Port Act, which ordered the port closed to shipping while the town made restitution for the tea dumped in the harbor during the Boston Tea Party. Next came still more ominous legislation. The Massachusetts Government Act altered the colony's old constitution. Henceforth, the governor's council would be appointed by the king rather than elected by the assembly, and town meetings would be held only once a year except by permission of the governor. An Administration of Justice Act provided that any government or customs officer indicted for murder could be tried in England, beyond control of local juries. A New Quartering Act authorized the quartering of troops within a town (instead of in the barracks provided by a colony) whenever their commanding officer thought it desirable. To underline the full intent of this act, the British troops, with heavy reinforcements, were brought back to Boston from the fort in the harbor. General Thomas Gage, the commander in chief of all the North American troops, was also sent to act as governor of the colony.

The colonists dubbed these new measures the Intolerable Acts. The Quebec Act followed. Although this last act had no punitive intentions, the colonists thought it as ominous for the other colonies as those acts passed against Massachusetts. It gave the Province of Quebec a permanent government with no representative assembly, established French civil law, offered special protection to the Catholic Church (which was especially alarming to Protestant New England), and annexed the entire region west of the Appalachians and north of the Ohio to the Province of Quebec. New Englanders, who were beginning to migrate to that area in increasing numbers, had no desire to put themselves under the autocratic government in Quebec.

Lord North thought he could teach the Americans to respect the supremacy of Parliament. But the lessons the colonists learned, and the one drummed repeatedly into the ears of the 100 plus students in the Yale chapel, was that the supremacy of Parliament meant an end to the power of their own representative assemblies and courts, an end to the right to trial by jury, and an end to every political principle that they held dear.

The Committees of Correspondence, which had been organized throughout America during earlier disturbances, went into action. Boston had once been known throughout the colonies chiefly for its merchants' hard bargaining and its inhabitants' riotous behavior. Now the town received universal admiration and sympathy. The Committees of Correspondence arranged for an intercolonial congress to coordinate action against the Intolerable Acts. It met in Philadelphia in September 1774, the same September that young Noah entered Yale.

The First Continental Congress, in effect, asked Parliament to repeal the noxious laws. Parliament made a few conciliatory gestures, but they weren't nearly enough. During this period, Lord North and the king knew they faced rebellion, but they thought it was limited only to Massachusetts. They had no idea that the contagion had spread to Connecticut and to all the other colonies.

Yale differed little from the eight other colleges then functioning in the American colonies, except that it was probably more distressed financially than any of the others. Inept teaching, maladministration, and a musty curriculum resulted in a breakdown of discipline, a wave of student hell-raising, and a resistance to learning.

Student life at Yale on the eve of the Revolution was infinitely more regimented and circumscribed than now. As an all-male community, the college aimed at a kind of monastic life dedicated to learning. The authorities levied fines for many disciplinary breaches, imposed daily prayers on the students, and enforced a regimen of rising and retiring at early hours with few diversions during the day. An undergraduate on a typical academic day rose at 5:30 A.M., attended prayers and recitation until 7:30, ate breakfast and walked in good weather until 8:15, studied until 11, attended classes from 11 to 12, had dinner at noon, walked or exercised until 3, studied again until 6, went to prayers and had supper, and then talked with other students until bed at 9 P.M.

Three unkempt buildings on a treeless barren common made up the physical facilities, nicknamed the Brick Prison by students who objected to the rigid discipline. A brick chapel contained the auditorium, a dusty library of about 2,500 old and rarely consulted books, and a museum cluttered with moth-eaten stuffed birds and animals, fossils, stones, and philosophical apparatus. Connecticut Hall, where Webster roomed, still stands as a reminder of Yale's early architectural Americanism. The third building, called Old College, was wooden and painted blue, and it was so rickety that it had to be razed in 1782. It served as dormitory, recitation hall, dining hall, and buttery where students could buy extra food, beer, cider, and metheglin (fermented honey and water). These beverages, considered soft drinks in the eighteenth century, were provided in an effort to keep undergraduates from drinking hard liquor in their rooms.

Repressing the animal spirits of 140 postadolescents, however, proved too much for the faculty of only two professors (including the president) and four or five tutors. Records of disciplinary actions overflow with fines for pulling out the bung of a barrel of cider stored by an unpopular tutor in the cellar of Connecticut Hall, upending the president's privy, traveling to college on the Sabbath, mimicking the president as he conducted prayers in chapel, and stealing chickens and eating the loot in the dormitory.

The students slept and studied in their rooms in Old College or Connecticut Hall. They split their own wood, built their own fires, and slipped shivering out of doors to visit the pump or the necessary. Everyone ate in the commons from pewter utensils (students weren't trusted with glass or crockery) under the vigilant eyes of the faculty who tried to keep order and who were often unsuccessful in discouraging the throwing of bread and bones and the loud complaining about the quality of the food.

When available, meat was served for dinner at the noon meal with two potatoes apiece, and sometimes a broth was served with a pudding, called Injun pudding, which was probably made of cornmeal. The pudding was boiled in the broth and eaten before the meat. The students also had cabbage and turnip and dandelion greens, with plenty of cider passed around in pewter cans from which all drank in turn. Brown bread and milk made up the supper in the evening. Judging from Webster's later abstemious eating habits, we can guess that supper was his favorite meal.

Yale President Daggett had trouble with discipline, a factor that may have contributed to the fact that his presidential status remained temporary for a decade until he resigned in 1777. But his tenure was distinguished by a succession of brilliant young tutors and by a move that made the school more democratic socially (although democratic would not have been used then, because it had the connotation in those days of mob rule). Daggett changed the practice of listing students by rank according to supposed family distinction or respectability, and used instead the more democratic alphabetical order. The spirit of democracy also surfaced in the 1768 formation of a new literary society, the Brothers of Unity, to which Noah, Jr., belonged. Its name indicated a freer spirit than that of the older Linonian Society which dated from 1754. It also had a circulating library of a few hundred books that were generally more modern than those in the main library.

Daggett was unpopular in spite of, or perhaps because of, his difficulties with discipline. Students grew increasingly restive, and he resigned in March 1777. Dr. Ezra Stiles was elected to succeed him, but he didn't move to the college until 1778. Although Webster's class had the benefit of his much improved administration and leadership for only three months, young Noah soon came to know and respect him, keeping the same high regard for him for the rest of his life. Stiles, too, proved to be a patriot of the Trumbull-Dwight stamp.

The Latin and Greek languages, philosophy, mathematics, and theology made up most of the uninspired curriculum. One modern course was a timid foray into natural science, but it didn't even mention the new chemistry of Joseph Priestley. In 1771 Dwight and Trumbull had begun an attempt to liberalize the course of study, with such radical suggestions as substituting English composition and the review of English literature for some of the work in Latin and Greek. Yet progress was hindered by the increasing disruptions of the imminent war. The rigorous content of the out-dated curriculum, nevertheless, developed minds that were later to wrestle successfully with some of the great problems of the era.

Besides Webster, the 40-man class of 1778 included many who were later to become distinguished: Joel Barlow, the poet and minister to France; Zephaniah Stewart, chief justice of Connecti-cut's Supreme Court; Alexander Wolcott and Abraham Bishop, both active in Jeffersonian politics; Oliver Wolcott, Jr., successor to Hamilton as secretary of the treasury and afterward governor of Connecticut; Uriah Tracy, a United States senator from Connecti-cut; and Josiah Meigs, president of the University of Georgia.

Professors at Yale donned black robes, white wigs, and high cocked hats. Tutors wore silk gowns and chevrons to set them apart from the graduate students. The three upper classes appeared in gowns of camlet (a combination of goat's hair and silk). The fresh-men alone wore street dress. They were supposed to serve the needs of the upper classmen and faculty, a tradition fiercely re-sented and largely ignored by Webster's class.

Joseph Buckminster, the tutor of the 1778 class, was an amia-ble man with a passion for accuracy that appealed to young Noah if not to some of his classmates. Noah, in fact, became one of Buckminster's pets. Because Buckminster was more than a little jealous of Dwight, he resigned when Ezra Stiles was elected presi-dent of Yale, irked at the favor Dwight enjoyed with both the students and the new president. Buckminster viewed his association with Webster's class "with particular satisfaction," although he re-gretted "the independent spirit" of the students. He finished his life as a New England pastor.

The class unsuccessfully petitioned to have Dwight their tutor for the senior year following Buckminster's resignation. But Dwight, too, had resigned to become chaplain in the revolutionary army.

Noah Webster's last three years at the college were frequently disrupted by the fortunes of war, epidemics of disease, and short-ages of food. He got through his freshman year in 1774–75 with little interruption. Word of the Battle of Lexington arrived in New Haven on April 21, 1775. Although exempt from military service, the students formed a company and drilled on the green with the New Haven militia. Webster had learned to play the flute, a favored instrument with the family's males for several generations, and with it paced the drillers.

Webster's studies during his second year in 1775–76 included geography, as well as the conventional divinity, Latin, Greek, rhetoric, and geometry. The progress of the war interested the students more, as did Thomas Paine's inflammatory essays.

When General Washington and Major General Charles Lee reached New Haven on their way to Cambridge to take charge of the American Army, the students and two uniformed companies escorted them out of town on June 29. Years later, Webster recalled, "it fell to my humble lot to lead the company with music." His enemies years later pounced on that statement as another example of his vainglory.

Two days after the Declaration of Independence, fellow classmate Joel Barlow wrote his mother: "The students are sensibly affected with the unhappy situation of public affairs, which is a great hindrance to their studies."

In August 1776, an epidemic of typhoid fever caused the college's dismissal. Webster rushed to West Hartford where his brother Abraham, who had been a member of an abortive expedition to Canada, was convalescing from smallpox. When Abraham had recovered, Noah accompanied him back to his company stationed at the head of Lake Champlain in New York. On this trip, young Noah saw firsthand the discomforts of soldiering—mosquitoes, men sick from dysentery and fever, and all the myriad dangers and uncertainties. This and a later brief experience as a full-fledged soldier led Noah to identify closely with Revolutionary War veterans for the rest of his life. The events confirmed him still more firmly in his lifelong patriotism and nationalism.

At the start of Noah's junior year in November 1776, he found Yale so crowded that four students had to live together in each of the larger rooms in Connecticut Hall and two in each smaller room. This overcrowding probably taught a more dramatic lesson than did the recitations in Latin, Greek, natural philosophy, astronomy, and divinity. Food grew so scarce that the college had to dismiss the students on December 10. The students returned on January 7, 1777, but the same problem forced dismissal again on

March 29. Writing later about this time, Webster reported that "the farmers cut cornstalks, crushed them in cider mills, and then boiled the juice down to a syrup, as a substitute for sugar."

During this enforced vacation, the 19-year-old suffered smallpox, then the scourge of the colonies. Although his fair, ruddy complexion was not left pockmarked, he complained frequently of ill-health from this time on until his death. The disease and the poor diet possibly damaged a constitution that had been robust until then.

In April 1777, a British force that had sailed up the Hudson and landed at Peekskill, New York, raided Danbury, Connecticut, to destroy valuable Continental stores. This event and the food shortage led Yale to seek new temporary quarters where food would be more plentiful and the students safer than in New Haven, which was considered an eventual target for the British. The seniors under Dwight went to Wethersfield; the juniors under Buckminster, and the sophomores under Professor Nehemia Strong, the mathematics instructor, went to Glastonbury; the freshmen under Abraham Baldwin reported to Farmington. Young Noah resumed his studies in May, rooming with Ichabod Wetmore at the home of Asa Talcott.

The Danbury raid seemed like a college prank compared with what developed in the summer of 1777. Britain's General Burgoyne spread terror throughout northeastern New York and Vermont. He intended to move down the Hudson to Albany and then meet the British army from New York City. The two armies then planned to set up posts from New York to Canada and cut off New England and New York from the rest of the colonies.

In every Connecticut town the militia organized to reinforce the beleaguered Continental troops along the Hudson River. Noah Webster, Sr., now a captain in West Hartford, drilled the men over age 40, in addition to a few volunteers who included his sons, Abraham and Charles. Yale classes ended on September 10, in time for Noah, Jr., to join his father and brothers.

The militia went up the east bank of the Hudson, heading for Albany. Before they reached the city, a courier rode by, shouting, "Burgoyne is taken!" The British general had been bottled up near Saratoga and had been forced to surrender, the army from New York City having failed to arrive.

Young Webster then and later thought this to be the turning point in the war. "Well might every American who had shared in the conflict, or who was hastening to meet the foe, exult in such a victory," he wrote. This safe, brief experience as a militiaman constituted his only real experience as a soldier, but it enabled him to return to New Haven as a veteran for his senior year late in November 1777.

Webster's last year of study included reading *On Human Understanding* by the philosopher John Locke, whose ideas on religion the students were supposed to refute. Actually, Noah and others found much in it to challenge their orthodox Calvinism. The other three classes remained in the country. Problems of food and war again forced dismissal of the college, this time from February 24 to June 23, 1778. Young Noah probably returned home during this period to help on the farm.

When college resumed, the new president, Dr. Ezra Stiles, took over the senior class. He electrified the members with his erudition, his zeal for learning, and his unusually liberal views on both religious and political subjects. He also controlled them shrewdly, although he called them a "bundle of wild fire." He later remarked that "at best, the diadem of a president is a crown of thorns." In Dwight and Trumbull the students had encountered superior minds; they met another in Dr. Stiles, though only for three months.

At the commencement on September 9, 1778, Webster gave the Cliosophic Oration in English, an honor indicating that he had placed high in the top quarter of the class. He and his classmates received the bachelor of arts degree.

In his diary for July 1778, Dr. Stiles noted: "The seniors disputed forensically this day in twofold question, 'Whether the destruction of the Alexandrine Library, and the ignorance of the Middle Ages caused by the inundation of the Goths and Vandals, were events unfortunate to literature?' They disputed inimitably well; particularly Barlow, Swift, Webster, Gilbert, Meigs, Sage, etc."

A college education in those days might compare with a 10th-grade education in today's good public schools. Furthermore, the college of the late eighteenth century had no organized athletics, no college weekends, and few diversions in a town of only 8,000 inhabitants to mar the sobriety of college life.

Not much survives about Webster's personal college experience. None of his letters from that era has been found, nor does his name show in the extant college records. From the available material it is apparent that he enjoyed the respect of his college classmates. In 1776 Zephaniah Swift wrote Noah Webster in an Addisonian vein on the difficulty of becoming both a man of the world and man of letters. He told Webster: "Your opportunities and the time you spend with the ladies will enable you to reach both."

So Noah already showed his delight in feminine parties and dances. But he also showed himself as a conscientious student and a hard worker. He mastered Latin and Greek so thoroughly that in his old age he could still write letters in Latin to his favorite granddaughter, Emily Fowler. Yet Webster didn't end his education at Yale, for he spent the rest of his life studying.

Chapter 3

THEN CAME INDEPENDENCE

After graduation from Yale, young Noah Webster came home to West Hartford, and to a shock. Instead of his father giving him further financial support to study law, as he had hoped, the elder Webster gave him an eight-dollar bill of the Continental currency, so depreciated that it was worth about two dollars in silver.

"Take this," Noah, Sr., said. "I can do no more for you."

Noah, Jr., retired to his room for three days to meditate and read. Among the books he studied was Samuel Johnson's *Rambler*. One sentence remained in his memory as an axiom by which he tried to live for the rest of his life: "To fear no eye, to suspect no tongue, is the greatest prerogative of innocence, an exemption granted only to invariable virtue."

Probably Abraham and Charles had influenced their father's decision, because neither had received comparable educational advantages. The farm, already mortgaged to pay for Noah's Yale education, could barely support the family in those war-torn times.

Noah Webster was right about the importance of Burgoyne's surrender at Saratoga. It had convinced the French they could back a winner, so they signed an alliance with the fledgling nation on February 6, 1778. Even before the alliance, the Americans had depended heavily on aid from France. The victory at Saratoga, for example, would have been impossible without French supplies. The French financial aid helped to bolster American credit when Congress, without the right to tax, had to finance the war with handouts from the states and with money manufactured on the printing presses.

After Saratoga the British fought a cautious war. General William Howe, comfortable in Philadelphia during the winter of 1777–78, did not bother to attack Washington's wretched forces starving and freezing in their nearby winter quarters at Valley Forge. In the spring Sir Henry Clinton replaced the languid Howe. Uncertain as to where France would strike, the British high command decided to play safe and ordered Clinton to withdraw from Philadelphia to New York. There he was to plan a major campaign in the South where the strategists thought the loyalists would lend a decisive hand.

At Valley Forge, as milder weather came, Washington's forces thawed out. Baron Friedrich Von Steuben, a Prussian idealist and experienced military man, arrived to help drill the ragged army into shape. Supplies improved, and so did morale.

Nothing decisive happened, however, for a year and a half. The French Navy had more important matters to attend to in the Caribbean, and Washington didn't dare attempt a broad attack on the British, now safe in New York with British Navy support, unless the English fleet could be drawn off. Various minor engagements between small British and American forces occurred in Pennsylvania and the South, but the strategic center remained around New York.

After some successes in Georgia, Clinton decided in 1779 to launch a major southern campaign. Accordingly, he left a force in New York equal to Washington's, and withdrew British troops from Newport, thus leaving New England free of all English soldiers for the first time since the Revolution had begun. In December 1779, he sailed with an expeditionary force of 8,000 to Charles Town (Charleston), South Carolina. He took the place on May 12, 1780. The Carolinas now lay open to British conquest. Still cautious, Clinton left Lord Charles Cornwallis in command and returned to New York. The Americans kept picking away at Cornwallis who ill-advisedly decided to conquer Virginia in early 1781, perhaps because he had had little success winning the Carolinas or Georgia.

He settled at Portsmouth and later at Yorktown. Both lay on the seacoast, the only safe place for a British army in America. Yet the English would remain safe only as long as their navy commanded the nearby sea. Without naval support Cornwallis could be cut off from his own forces remaining in Charles Town and Savannah and from Clinton's army in New York.

Clinton and Washington still waited each other out. In May 1781, Washington's patience finally paid off with the news that Admiral De Grasse with 20 warships was sailing from France for the West Indies and would detach part of his force to assist the Americans. At first, Washington planned to attack New York, but then word came that De Grasse was headed for the Chesapeake with his entire fleet. Furthermore, he could stay only a short time. Washington then decided to abandon the planned New York campaign and to dash south for a coup against Cornwallis.

In the meantime, De Grasse bested the British fleet in the Chesapeake, and its remnants fled back to New York. Washington hurried toward Yorktown with 5,700 Continentals, 3,100 militia, and 7,000 French. On October 19, 1781, when an English relief fleet was already under way from New York, Cornwallis gave up. With the bands playing "The World Turned Upside Down," 7,000 British troops stacked their arms in surrender.

After the defeat at Yorktown, most Englishmen were ready to give up the colonies even though George III wanted the war to continue. When Lord North was forced from office on March 20, 1782, the king had to accept a ministry that favored peace. Preliminary articles of peace were signed on November 30, 1782. The final treaties were signed in Paris on September 3, 1783, and the first British troops left New York on November 25. The Declaration of Independence was at last a description, not a wish.

Although the tide of war had shifted south of New England in 1778, this was still no time for a young man to start a career. Of course, Noah, Jr., knew this. He emerged from three days in his room, still resolved to study law, but he would earn his living by teaching until conditions improved. He may have had some consolation in the fact that other classmates faced comparable obstacles. His friend, Joel Barlow, wrote him: "You and I are not the first in the world to have broken loose from college without friends and without fortune to push us into public notice. Let us show the world a few more examples of men standing upon their own merit and rising in spite of obstacles. . . . I have too much confidence in your merits, both as to greatness of genius and goodness of heart, to suppose that your actions are not to be conspicuous."

Noah went first to Glastonbury, where he had lived for part

of his junior year in college. He got a school for the winter term of 1778–79. No records survive of this experience, but his classmate Shabael Breed also taught at this time and complained: "I have taken upon me the important office of a schoolmaster—about 30 scholars, one-third Latin, who by their continual clamour open a scene of unbounded torment and external vexation. . . . It's a poor business, the wages not equivalent to a support, and the knowledge gained by it not worth a farthing. I shall soon dismiss it."

Neither did young Noah stay long in Glastonbury. By the spring of 1779 he had moved to Hartford where he got a job teaching in the Brick School House and lived with Oliver Ellsworth, later Chief Justice of the United States Supreme Court. Here Noah at last began studying his cherished law in Ellsworth's large library. He also helped Ellsworth in his law office. The strain of the times and the toil of teaching, studying, and working in the office took a toll on Noah's health. He began suffering from a vaguely described nervous problem that tormented him for the next two years. That may have been the reason he returned home in the fall of 1779 to teach in his native parish. His pay was probably no more than the going rate of the period, one pound to one pound and a half per month—much too little to go toward repaying the college bill of 120 pounds.

Although self-supporting, young Noah may not have had the wholehearted backing of his two brothers when he returned home. The winter of 1779–80 also remained memorable for its severity. He had to walk eight miles each day to and from school through snow that at times covered the fences. Such experiences contributed to his rising criticism of the quality of public education.

He wrote four essays on "the most usual defects of our country schools." While turgid and amateurish, these essays hold one's interest because they represent his first attempt at formulating an attitude toward elementary schools. "The general institution of schools in this country," he said, "is full proof that the inhabitants are convinced of their utility and importance." But, he added, "people never misapply their economy so much, as when they make mean provision for the education of children." School houses remained in poor condition, even worse than when he attended them as a pupil. And "the absolute impossibility of obtaining books" was inexcusable, he wrote. Especially significant is his refutation of the widely observed motto, "Spare the rod and spoil the child." On the contrary, Webster said, "the pupil should have nothing to discourage him." He also emphasized the importance of the pupils' health and comfort—radical ideas for that time.

At this point, Noah, Jr., found himself at the early stages of an experimental period running from 1776 to 1789, when the former British colonial settlers were trying to discover their nationality—politically, socially, and educationally. Progress proved more rapid in the first two areas than in the third.

Yet the assumption that widespread education was desirable had taken hold with a revival of public schooling, which had lapsed seriously from about 1776 to 1778. Barely 21 years of age, Webster began a program for reform that took him more than half a century to achieve even moderate success. Yet he never gave up. At the beginning, he emphasized the humanitarian and economic aspects of the school problem. Later, he added both religious and democratic ideals to push through his reforms.

Law remained his main ambition, however. In the summer of 1780, he jumped at the chance to move to Litchfield, Connecticut, to assist Jedidiah Strong, a justice of the quorum and recorder of deeds for Litchfield County. He resumed his study of law, probably under Strong but perhaps with Tapping Reeve, founder of the famous Litchfield Law School.

At the March term of court, Webster and about 20 others applied for admission to the bar. All were refused. The reason is unknown, but it may have been fear of overcrowding the profession. That didn't stop Noah, who went to Hartford where, examined and approved, he was admitted to practice on April 13, 1781. In less than three years from his graduation from Yale, he achieved his goal, another early example of the persistence and dogged determination that characterized him.

Americans of the late eighteenth century were a highly litigious people, and a horde of lawyers catered to their wishes. Most cases proved trivial and involved debt. Thomas Jefferson, for example, averaged only $2,000 per year from his practice. In 1773, his peak year, he dealt with more than 500 cases, most of them concerned with minor matters.

Webster joined an ancient profession that was, unfortunately, no longer quite honorable, largely because of the dunning tactics

used by lawyers against debtors. One critic of lawyers wrote: "They foment more wrath, evil speaking and bitterness among neighbourhoods than their reverend fathers could heal, if they should attempt it. And if sin be, as some clerical wiseacres have asserted, for the glory of God, these lawyers work day and night for his glory. Without dignity of manners they blacken the courts and clients and witnesses and each other most unmercifully. They consider the receipt of fees as justifying them in pursuing to utter destruction an honest family by a claim which they know to be unrighteous."

Yet, the young man could now write his name Noah Webster, Junior, Esquire, Attorney at Law. He evidently liked the ring of it because he henceforth signed it that way often. More Yale graduates entered law by the 1770s than any other profession. The college originally prepared most of its alumni for the ministry. In 1748, nearly half the graduates became clerics, nearly one-third in 1758, one-fourth in 1768, but only one-tenth by 1778. By that date, medicine had become the second most popular profession for graduates.

Although Noah Webster, Junior, Esquire, Attorney at Law could now practice law, he didn't in those economically depressed times. He decided to keep on teaching. Already, in fact, he embarked on a course of multicareers, typical in that multitalented age.

On October 7, 1780, the traitor Benedict Arnold had written an article to the inhabitants of America, justifying his actions. Webster wrote a moderate and reasoned reply that ran shortly after in *The Connecticut Courant*—his first known appearance in the public prints. Men of education commonly contributed to the periodicals of that day. The printer, also usually the editor, encouraged the practice to fill his columns. There was no wire-service copy, and little local news reporting as we know it today. While most contributors received no pay, well-known correspondents demanded it. Perhaps the hard-pressed Webster saw this as an eventual source of income, a hope that would one day become a reality.

The years 1781 and 1782 did not seem to go particularly well for young Webster. He couldn't pursue law; his teaching experiences met with continual frustrations; and he suffered an acute social embarrassment. He had decided to return to schoolmastering, an occupation for which he knew he was temperamentally and educationally suited, and wished to start his own academy, choosing the town of Sharon in Connecticut's Litchfield County as its site. Many New Yorkers had settled there because the British in the summer of 1781 still occupied the city. The New Yorkers in Sharon included the families of Robert Gilbert Livingston and Mrs. Theodosia Prevost, who later became Mrs. Aaron Burr. Webster published this ad in *The Connecticut Courant* on June 1, 1781:

> The subscriber, desirous of promoting Education, so essential to the interest of a free people, proposes immediately to open a school at Sharon, in which young Gentlemen and Ladies may be instructed in Reading, Writing, Mathematicks, the English Language, and if desired, the Latin and Greek Languages—in Geography, Vocal Music & at the moderate price of Six Dollars and two thirds per quarter per Scholar. The strictest attention will be paid to the studies, the manners and the morals of youth by the public's very humble servant, Noah Webster, Jun.

The school opened July 1 with pupils from many of Sharon's best families. Young Webster might have founded one of the famous New England academies that survive to this day, but he ran afoul of Juliana Smith and Rebecca Pardee. He cultivated these and other pretty young ladies at a singing school he conducted in the evening (a common institution for genteel women then) and at a literary society established by Juliana. She was the 19-year-old sister of John Cotton Smith, later to be a governor of Connecticut, in whose home Webster may have held both the elementary and singing schools.

Young Noah was now above ordinary height, slim, neat in dress, his unruly red hair as controlled as possible. Although his chin jutted a little too much for some tastes, many of the young ladies evidently thought him handsome. Perhaps even the young schoolmaster thought himself good-looking as he gazed into his steel mirror.

Unfortunately, he gave no such impression to Juliana. To her, he seemed vain, pompous, and unduly proud of his honors. In September 1781, he had received the master of arts degree from Yale for his dissertation. For the October issue of *The Clio,* a manuscript magazine that contained society members' literary efforts, he had contributed a stilted fable with an unexceptionable moral lesson.

Juliana Smith wrote:

Mr. Webster has not the excuse of youth, (I think he must be fully twenty-two or three), but his essays—don't be angry, Jack,—are as young as yours or brother Tommy's while his reflections are as prosy as those of our horse, your namesake, would be if they were written out. Perhaps more so, for I truly believe, judging from the way *Jack Horse* looks 'round at me sometimes, when I am on his back, that his thoughts of the human race and their conduct towards his own might be well worth reading. At least they would be all *his own,* and that is more than can be said of N. W.'s. In conversation he is even duller than in writing, if that is possible, but he is a painstaking man and a hard student. Papa says he will make his mark.

Besides having to suffer Juliana's tart tongue, Noah faced the problem of Rebecca Pardee, who was a beautiful girl. He proposed marriage. She had, however, another suitor, a major in the army who chose this time to come home. The poor girl couldn't make up her mind. A family council couldn't resolve it either, so the embarrassing matter had to go before the church elders, who decided in favor of the major. Evidently he had staked his claim earlier.

Young Noah abruptly closed his school on October 9, and left Sharon. No contemporary accounts have surfaced to testify about his reasons, but it is likely that this stiff, self-conscious introvert thought himself mortally wounded by both Rebecca and Juliana. (Interestingly, Webster was to marry another Rebecca and to name a daughter Juliana.)

Perhaps his nervous disorder warped his judgment or made it impossible for him to continue teaching. He probably lived in West Hartford through the winter of 1781–82, allegedly seeking "commercial employment." That plan, alone, serves as a measure of the distraction in both his own life and that of his country. In those times, a college-educated man went into one of the professions and only rarely into business or any other calling, unless he had family connections already established in it. Nor did he do manual work, like farming or printing. If Noah had early learned something about the mechanical or even accounting aspects of printing, he would have saved himself much trouble later.

During this winter of recuperation and job hunting, Noah Webster continued his private studies. One of his positive accomplishments at Sharon had been to learn French under the tutelage

of a Genevan Huguenot minister, John Peter Tetard. Tetard may
also have introduced him to the fascinating mysteries of comparative grammar. Webster had also probably begun studying German,
Italian, and Spanish—at least the first two languages under the
multilingual Swiss.

A knowledge of French introduced him in depth for the first
time to French philosophy, especially that of Jean Jacques Rousseau. Tom Paine's inflammatory essays in *The Crisis* took on deeper
meaning after he had read Rousseau's *Social Contract.* The two
exhilarated him. They embodied the ideas and ideals of eighteenth-
century liberalism, which Webster fully embraced at this time. The
characteristic ideas of this movement were that creativity was inherent in the individual, that the creative genius of man could be
directed for social progress, that the lines of human progress could
be determined, and that the continuous development of the human
race through scientific control was the only valid function of institutions. In the past, institutions had resulted from chance or accident,
argued Rousseau. Now, said Paine, an opportunity existed in
America for the scientific development of organizations that would
be flexible and useful to forward common interests.

Democracy implied the creation of intelligent citizens who
would clearly see their responsibility to develop the proper institutions of government and whatever else would be needed. Thus, an
educational organization must develop to assure creative democracy. This would free man from the limitations of superstition and
archaic institutions. Education would make inevitable a scientific,
objective, experimental attitude that would lead to creative innovation and that would energize reconstruction of everything related
to man's progress, and the direction for such progress could in this
way be scientifically determined.

Benjamin Franklin had brought Paine to America as the pam-
phleteer for the American Revolution. Paine wrote his essays while
he sat by the camp fires of the Revolutionary Army; others read his
essays aloud to all the soldiers by Washington's order. A sentence
in Paine's Letter to the People of France gives the key to his
underlying message: "Let us punish by instructing rather than by
revenge." Webster took this to heart, plus. the corollary that the
abuses of mankind rested ultimately in ignorance and that enlight-
enment was the sure remedy for oppression.

The Revolution had intoxicated Webster and his fellow students at Yale; now a closer reading of Paine and others helped him to articulate more clearly these principles underlying the war against England. These principles include—

1. separation from Great Britain, stated early in 1776 by Paine's *Common Sense.*
2. the natural basis of society, introduced by Rousseau and perhaps most succinctly expressed by James Otis in his *Speech on Writs of Assistance.* Otis asserted that the rights of life, liberty and property were "derived only from nature and the author of nature; and that they were inherent, inalienable, and indefeasible by any laws, pacts, contracts, covenants or stipulations which man could devise." He added that "every man, merely natural, was an independent sovereign, subject to no law, but the law written on his heart and revealed to him by his Maker, in the constitution of his nature."
3. that the people are the source of power. Many writers argued for this, notably Rousseau.
4. the inalienable rights of life, liberty, and happiness. Again, many sources argued for this.
5. the right of the people to determine their form of government. This follows naturally from the previous principles.

Young Noah Webster gave such ideas his own interpretation in print. A series of four essays, "Observations on the Revolution of America," appeared in *The New York–Packet,* beginning January 31, 1782. They are his first published writings on nationalism. Early evidence of his later polemical bent appears in such a passage as this: "Great Britain, having experienced the inefficacy of fleets and armies to support her illegal claims . . . is making use of sophistry, fraud, and bribery to disunite the Americans and overturn our independence. We are harassed with manifestos, proclamations, foreign letters of disappointed courtiers, and a thousand fugitive publications of mercenary printers, generals, governors, and anonymous scribblers." This referred to proclamations by Sir Henry Clinton attempting to persuade the Americans to lay down their arms and to other propaganda forays by the British trying to plant suspicion of French duplicity and intrigue in the minds of Americans.

In his second essay Webster explained the legal justification for the Declaration of Independence, arguing "that the King of Great Britain, having attempted to impose some unconstitutional and oppressive laws upon the colonies, having withdrawn his protection and confiscated their property, had thus forfeited all right to their allegiance." In this, Webster almost quoted Paine directly.

The third essay refuted the notion that "America could never be happy under any other than British government." So great is the commercial and enterprising spirit, he argued, that America will have "more tons of shipping in traffic than any power in Europe." The 23-year-old schoolmaster proved to be prophetic when he wrote these words, a characteristic he demonstrated many times throughout his life.

In his fourth essay, he attacked attempts to inflame moral and religious prejudices. "They tell us," he wrote, "that a separation from Great Britain will introduce and accelerate the progress of luxury, and that the protestant religion will lose ground, if not be totally extirpated, through the influence of a popish ally. To liberal minds, these dangers are phantoms, mere illusions of a distempered imagination." Webster concludes rather bombastically:

America sees the absurdities—she sees the kingdoms of Europe, disturbed by wrangling sectaries, or their commerce, population and improvements of every kind cramped and retarded, because the human mind like the body is fettered 'and bound fast by the cords of policy and superstition': She laughs at their folly and shuns their errors: She founds her empire upon the idea of an universal toleration: She admits all religions into her bosom—she secures the sacred rights of every individual: and (astonishing absurdity to Europeans!) she sees a thousand discordant opinions live in the strictest harmony of friendship. This privilege of an unprecedented toleration must incite nations into her dominions; preserve a tranquility in society that must cast a shade upon all the Hierarchies of the earth—it will finally raise her to a pitch of greatness and lustre, before which the glory of ancient Greece and Rome shall dwindle to a point, and the splendor of modern Empires shall fade into obscurity.

The first essay was reprinted in the *Salem Gazette,* so Webster found currency around Boston, as well as in New York and Connecticut. Yet, he probably got paid little or nothing for these efforts. He needed a job. In the spring of 1782 Noah returned to Sharon to try to reestablish his school. He published an advertisement that is notable because it describes a secondary school of that period and because it shows his progress in developing a theory and philosophy of education:

On the first of May will be opened at Sharon in Connecticut, a school, in which children may be instructed, not only in the common arts of reading, writing, and arithmetic, but in any branch of Academical literature. The little regard that is paid to the literary improvement of females, even among people of rank and fortune, and the general inattention to the grammatical purity and elegance of our native language, are faults in the education of youth that more gentlemen and ladies have taken pains to censure than to correct. Any young gentlemen and ladies, who wish to acquaint themselves with the English language, geography, vocal music, &c., may be waited upon at particular hours for that purpose. The price of board and tuition will be from six to nine shillings, lawful money per week, according to the age and studies of the Scholar; no pains will be spared to render the school useful.

The school never reopened, probably because parents had already made other arrangements and looked askance at a teacher who had so abruptly quit the previous October.

Although Webster had regressed rather than progressed on the material side of his life during 1781–82, he had grown intellectually. Furthermore, he had an idea, and it warmed and nurtured his natural optimism as he headed south and west to the hamlet of Goshen in Orange County, New York.

PART TWO

Webster the Educator

Chapter 4

SPELLING IT OUT

Noah Webster arrived in Goshen, New York, with 75 cents in his pocket, but the idea for a fortune in his head. The idea was for a spelling book, and it did ultimately net a fortune. Unfortunately, just part of it went to him; probably more of it went to unscrupulous printers and booksellers. Yet, the modest book, whose first edition contained only 119 pages and cost just 14 pence, launched him irrevocably along the path of writing and teaching. It was the first American best-seller. It led its author to become the father of the American copyright law. It taught generations of Americans a uniform spelling and a fairly consistent manner of pronunciation. It preached a cultural Declaration of Independence. And it gave its author his own freedom for the first time. Now, nearly two centuries after the first edition appeared in 1783, no one can know for certain all of Noah's motives for preparing the book. One of them, however, must have been to earn money. He needed it badly to support himself and to repay his father for his college education. Teachers earned a mere pittance, even by the standards of those times. He needed to supplement his income.

Noah Webster also needed another profession. Nobody in his right mind then wanted to teach public secondary school for long. Besides the low pay and poor facilities, a teacher had to endure a place near the bottom of the social scale. Wealthy plantation owners were known to have employed English ex-convicts to give their children the rudiments of the three Rs. Instructors seldom stayed long in one position, so impermanence was still another undesirable quality.

Yet Webster loved to teach. If ever a born teacher existed, it was he. For him, teaching had already become as natural as breathing. In one way or another for the rest of his life he found ways to teach, usually other than in the classroom.

The speller proved to be his first successful form of teaching outside the classroom. The idea for it may have first come during his West Hartford school experience when he had been frustrated by the shortage of textbooks. He probably worked on it at Sharon and during his period of unemployment in West Hartford the following winter. He finished the book at Goshen.

At Goshen young Webster taught at the Farmer's Hall Academy, to which Henry Wisner, a signer of the Declaration of Independence, the Reverend Dr. Nathaniel Kerr, and others sent their children. At least one former pupil from Sharon, Jonas Platt, followed him to Goshen, testimony to his excellence as an instructor. Although Webster received silver instead of the depreciated Continental paper for the first time, his pay barely supported him.

He spent all his spare time on the spelling book; for still another powerful force drove him in his task. This force was his patriotic zeal. Although it may seem strange that a spelling book could serve as an instrument to further nationalism, Noah achieved this, too. He highlighted his goal in his introduction:

Previously to the late war, America preserved the most unshaken attachment to Great-Britain: The king, the constitution, the laws, the commerce, the fashions, the books, and even the sentiments of Englishmen were implicitly supported to be the best on earth: not only their virtues and improvements, but their prejudices, their errours, their vices and their follies were adopted by us with avidity. But by a concurrence of those powerful causes that effect almost instantaneous revolutions in states, the political views of America have suffered a total change. She now sees a mixture of profound wisdom and consummate folly in the British constitution; a ridiculous compound of freedom and tyranny in their laws; .... She views the vices of that nation with abhorrence, their errours with pity, and their follies with contempt.

While the Americans stand astonished at their former delusion and enjoy the pleasure of a final separation from their insolent sovereigns, it becomes their duty to attend to the arts of peace, and particularly to the interests of literature; to see if there be not some errours to be corrected, some defects to be supplied, and some improvements to be introduced into our system of education, as well as those of civil policy.

Thus, Webster adroitly combined patriotism with the ABCs. The times were ripe for the new venture. Thomas Dilworth had earlier combined a speller, grammar, and reader in his work entitled *New Guide to the English Tongue,* which had been universally adopted in the New England schools by 1765. It had first been published in London in 1740, and it bristled with references to British royalty and English geography that now served no purpose whatever for the new American citizens. Furthermore, Dilworth was inaccurate, as Noah Webster pointed out in his speller's introduction and at every other opportunity until he had driven his rival from the market. Webster described it as the most imperfect guide in use in schools, even though its authority had become as "sacred as the tradition of the Jews or the Mahometan Bible." He added, "one half of the work is totally useless, and the other half, defective and erroneous." Nevertheless, Webster's speller looked suspiciously like Dilworth's section on spelling. True, he abandoned most of Dilworth's religious materials, substituting precepts of the Poor Richard variety, exhortations to lead good lives, and proverbs and maxims:

> When wine is in, wit is out.
> A good cow may have a bad calf.
> You must not buy a pig in a poke.
> Let not your tongue cut your throat.
> He that lies down with dogs must rise up with fleas.

Noah Webster gave good advice to children on managing their school time, on developing good habits, and on how to achieve success:

> A wise child loves to learn his book; but the fool would choose to play with toys.
> Sloth keeps such a hold of some clowns that they lie in bed when they should go to school; but a boy that wants to be wise will drive sleep far from him.
> Love him that loves his book, and speaks good words, and does no harm, for such a friend may do thee good all the days of thy life.

The reading lessons "of easy words to learn [sic] children to read and know their duty" began with Dilworth's first sentence:

No man may put off the law of God.
My joy is in his law all the day.
O may I not go in the way of sin.
Let me not go in the way of ill men.

Webster borrowed from another English speller by Daniel
Fenning the well-known story of Tommy and Harry, but he re-
wrote and shortened it. Although such material was lifted from
other sources, the American reorganized it and added new pages.
In essence, it was a new book, but along a familiar pattern, a shrewd
move that probably contributed to its success.

As the editions of the book came tumbling from the press,
Webster gradually introduced the spelling practices that distinguish
American spelling from the British to this day. He chose the ending
-*or* over -*our* in words like *honor* and *color;* he changed the -*re* to
-*er* in words like *theater* and *center;* he dropped many double conso-
nants in words like *traveler* and *wagon;* he established *s* rather than
c in such words as *defense;* and he dropped the final *k* in *public* and
music. He made current many spellings that today are characteristically American, such as *jail, plow, mold, draft,* and *ax,* instead of the
British *gaol, plough, mould, draught,* and *axe.*

The timing for the speller's introduction proved fortunate,
too. Spelling in late eighteenth-century America was a decidely
casual affair, even for the well educated. James Madison was, for his
time, an excellent speller, but even he in his notes on the Constitutional Convention in 1787 was apt to write *Rutlidge* instead of
Rutledge, Dickenson instead of *Dickinson,* the word *secresy* instead of
secrecy, and the word *probaly* instead of *probably.*

The Americans, self-conscious in their newfound independence, were ripe for guides on how to improve themselves. They
wanted people from other nations to respect then, not to laugh at
their inability to spell their own language. Webster expressed it this
way in the speller's introduction:

The author wishes to promote the honour and prosperity of the
confederated republics of America; and chearfully throws his mite into the
common treasure of patriotic exertions. This country must in some future
time, be as distinguished by the superiority of her literary improvements,
as she is already by the liberality of her civil and ecclesiastical constitutions.

. . . It is the business of *Americans* to select the wisdom of all nations, as the basis of her constitutions,—to avoid their errors,—to prevent the introduction of foreign vices and corruptions and check the career of her own,—to promote virtue and patriotism, to embellish and improve the sciences,—to diffuse an uniformity and purity of language,—to add superior dignity to this infant Empire and to human nature.

Noah completed the manuscript for the speller, which he tentatively titled *The American Instructor,* in Goshen during the summer of 1782; he carefully test-marketed it with the parents of his students. Their unanimous approval exhilarated him, lifting the depression that he felt when he wrote of the book: "I have sacrificed ease, pleasure, and health in the execution of it, and have nearly completed it. But such close application is too much for my constitution. I must relinquish the school or writing grammars."

In August 1782, the young author took his manuscript to Philadelphia, Princeton, New York, and New Haven to get criticism, endorsements, and copyright protection. He had with him letters of introduction, such as this one from Henry Wisner:

The Bearrer Mr. Noah Webster has taught a grammar School for sometime past in this place much to the Satisfaction of his Employers he is now doing some business in the literary way which will in opinion of good Judges be of Service to postarity he being a Stranger in Philadelphia may Stand in need of the assistance Some gentleman with whome you are acquainted he is a young gentleman whose morral as will political caracter is such as will render him worthy of your notice any favours which you may do him will be Serving the public and Accepted as a favour done your friend and very humble Servant, Henry Wisner.

At Princeton, Professor Samuel Stanhope Smith, later to be president of the university, suggested printing *-tion, -sion,* and *-cion* suffixes as one syllable, a suggestion Webster enthusiastically adopted, although it went against custom among the religious people of those days, since religious usage required that these suffixes be pronounced as two syllables.

In New Haven, Yale President Dr. Ezra Stiles made a suggestion for the title that Webster accepted but later regretted. Stiles opted for *A Grammatical Institute of the English Language* as a cover title for the three volumes the author planned—the speller, a grammar, and a reader. The title was probably drawn by analogy from

John Calvin's *Institutes.* Unfortunately, the pompous wording that Stiles suggested made the author vulnerable to charges of vanity. He later subordinated the unwieldy title for others. Two of the books, the speller and the reader, acquired the adjective American.

The tour that Noah Webster made in behalf of the speller depressed him because many of the men he called on thought the book too trivial for their attention. Although Benjamin Franklin and General Washington received him politely, they refused their endorsements on the grounds that they were not schoolmasters and therefore unqualified to pass on the merits of the manuscript.

Besides the somewhat disappointing response from learned and well-known figures of the day, Webster had trouble finding a publisher. Finally, he persuaded his friends Barzillai Hudson and George Goodwin, publishers of *The Connecticut Courant,* to print the book. They accepted his note (and a small one signed by Yale classmate Joel Barlow) for the printing bill in exchange for exclusive rights to produce succeeding editions.

Noah decided to return to Hartford to oversee the preparation of the speller. Although still little more than a village with 300 houses and 2,500 inhabitants, Hartford in 1783 was a metropolis compared with Goshen. As the gateway to the upper Connecticut River Valley, the state capital had grown rapidly as a staging and supply center for the thousands of immigrants who were pushing westward to the wilderness at the end of the war.

Both the lively social life and the pretty ladies also attracted the author who rented a room with John Trumbull, once a Yale tutor but now a prosperous lawyer. Webster considered trying law again —but once more decided against the overcrowded profession.

His books—and particularly the speller—kept him busy. It was first advertised for sale in the *Courant* of October 7, 1783. The 5,000-copy press run took nine months to sell. Second and third editions appeared in 1784 and sold much faster. In fact, it sold so well that Hudson & Goodwin faced an eventual dilemma: Whether to remain primarily a book printer or to concentrate on their newspaper, the *Courant.* They gradually opted for the *Courant,* relinquishing rights to the speller in all territory but New England, finally settling for Connecticut alone.

More than 50 impressions of the book appeared before 1800, some of them 25,000-copy runs. Another 100 impressions were run off by 1829 when the number of copies sold throughout the United States reached at least 20 million. By 1875 the total exceeded 75 million copies.

During Webster's lifetime, the book had many regional printers because slow transportation made it impractical for a single firm to service more than a limited area. This complicated publishing immensely and made extensive pirating relatively easy. Because the schoolmaster couldn't oversee the printing by every printer, many typographical errors crept in to agitate him.

A printer or a group of them sometimes underwrote a book, but usually the author in early America had to finance the publication himself. Occasionally, a fortunate author could find a patron or a group of patrons, called subscribers, to finance him. Webster tried all these methods during his career, but he usually ended by financing the publication himself.

These economic conditions, more than any other factors, sharply limited the publication of native American authors in the young Republic. As late as 1820, the British Sydney Smith taunted visiting Americans by pointing out that almost no one read an American book, but he would have had to exclude the paperback speller from his definition of book if he wished to remain accurate. By then the speller had been read by almost every literate American. For Webster it meant a triumph over almost insurmountable odds. In effect, he acted as his own publisher, dealing with the many vexatious and time-consuming problems that publishers now take care of. He even single-handedly overcame problems that publishers today never face: no national copyright laws and no established marketing outlets. His successful solutions to those two difficulties are so significant and so little-known that the next chapters will deal with them separately.

In 1783 the self-confident Webster probably had little idea of the torments that lay ahead of him as a publisher. Even if he had known, he undoubtedly would have persevered. When the odds piled up the highest against him, he always seemed to perform best.

The fact is that Part I of *A Grammatical Institution of the English Language* has probably sold nearly 100 million copies. It is, in fact, still printed and sold today. This extraordinary publishing venture became known later as *The American Spelling Book* or the *Blue-Backed Speller* because of the cover's color.

Marketed the way paperbacks are today in stores, Webster's speller was selling about one million copies a year at a time when the entire population of the country was less than 10 million. Homer Babbidge, master of Yale's Timothy Dwight College, says, "Its consequent influence upon the standard of American spelling is great beyond measurement." Historian Henry Steele Commager calls Webster, "certainly one of the fathers of American education," as a result of the speller. It has trained and strained more heads than any other book of its kind.

Although Noah Webster had a bonanza in his grasp, his frequent need for ready money led him to give ridiculously low terms. For $200 in cash, he granted Samuel Campbell, a New York printer, unlimited rights to sell in New York, New Jersey, North Carolina, South Carolina, and Georgia for five years. Campbell sold 20,000 copies a year and, before the contract ended, craftily stocked up with a printing of 100,000 copies. Webster lost $2,500 on that deal. He sold the same rights for 11 years for $1,000, again because he needed cash.

Many printers lied in their returns, paying only a fraction of what they really owed in royalties. Nathaniel Patten of Hartford, who bound Campbell's issues, spirited thousands of copies for himself and sold them in competition with authorized editions. Webster went to court in cases such as these and occasionally won, but the settlements were usually small because proof was difficult to get.

Nobody knows for sure how much of the speller's royalties actually reached Webster, but it is certain that only a small fraction of the possible total came to him. Nevertheless, that fraction proved his chief means of support for the rest of his life. Contemporary speculation put his income from the speller at $5,000 yearly during the 1820s, a guess that was probably too high.

A typical edition of the speller in the early 1800s consisted of easy-to-read articles on pronunciation, homilies, poems, catechisms, drills, vignettes, etc., as well as spelling lists.

Outstanding editions include *The American Spelling Book* of 1786 and the *Elementary Spelling Book* of 1829. Within four or five years of the 1829 edition, the speller had become standardized and known as the *Blue-Backed Speller* or "Webster's Old Spelling Book." From then on, it changed very little.

A typical standardized edition was plain—even homely—in outward appearance and contained 168 pages. A child of eight or nine was required to recite understandingly the opening sentence: "Language, in its more limited sense, is the expression of ideas by articulate sounds."

The use to which the speller was put is shown in this notice from a school in Danbury, Connecticut: "The advantages that small children obtain at this school may be easily imagined when the public are informed that those who spell go through the whole of Webster's spelling book twice a fortnight."

Alice Morse Earle's *Child Life in Colonial Days* gives a picture of how the book could have been used:

> The teaching of spelling in many schools was peculiar. The master gave out the word, with a blow of his strap on the desk as a signal for all to start together, and the whole class spelled out the word in syllables in chorus. The teacher's ear was so trained and accurate that he at once detected any misspelling. If this happened, he demanded the name of the scholar who made the mistake. If there was any hesitancy or refusal in acknowledgment, he kept the whole class until, by repeated trials of long words, accuracy was obtained. The roar of the many voices of the large school, all pitched in different keys, could be heard on summer days for a long distance. In many country schools the scholars not only spelled aloud but studied all their lessons aloud, as children in Oriental countries do today.

Alphabetized words were cunningly juxtaposed, as for example cider and crazy, in order to present a kind of subliminal lecture on temperance. That, plus the oral drills and pious maxims, helped sell the book to teachers and parents. But much of it appealed to the children, too, who enjoyed the spelling bees that developed from the drill. The speller's richness also lay in its woodcuts and the fables. The pictures came in the later editions. Woodcuts were expensive and engravers scarce. Webster probably wanted pictures in the very first edition, but either couldn't get them or couldn't afford them. As soon as possible, however, he added the famous drawings of the boy stealing apples, the crestfallen milkmaid, the partial judge, the entangled fox, the crafty cat, the patient fox, the cowardly friend, and the dog that foolishly kept bad company. While the author made additions and changes in content and spelling from time to time, he never altered the fables. The favorite was the first fable, lifted from Fenning's spelling book:

Of the Boy That Stole Apples

An old man found a rude boy upon one of his trees stealing apples, and desired him to come down; but the young sauce-box told him plainly he would not. Won't you? said the old man, then I will fetch you down; so he pulled up some turf or grass and threw at him; but this only made the youngster laugh, to think the old man should pretend to beat him down from the tree with grass only.

Well, well, said the old man, if neither words nor grass will do, I must try what virtue there is in stones. So the old man pelted him heartily with stones, which soon made the young chap hasten down from the tree and beg the old man's pardon.

Moral

If good words and gentle means will not reclaim the wicked, they must be dealt with in a more severe manner.

Webster made his most notable improvements over the Dilworth and Fenning spellers in syllabication and pronunciation, which through his efforts have become standard today in American and English usage.

In Dilworth such words as *cluster, habit,* and *nostril* had been divided as *clu-ster, ha-bit, no-stril.* Webster divided them as we do now: *clus-ter, hab-it,* and *nos-tril.* Thus, a beginner could pronounce and spell them more easily than when they were divided in the Dilworth manner.

Another change provoked hostility, but Webster stuck successfully to his guns, with the help of Princeton's Professor Smith. Religious usage required that the suffixes *-tion, -sion,* and *-cion* be pronounced as two syllables. Webster welded them into one, according to the civil usage.

The story goes that a Scottish Presbyterian elder in western Pennsylvania rode furiously into town one morning and called out: "Have ye heard the news, mon? Do ye ken what's gaen on? Here's a book by a Yankee lad called Webster, teaching the children clean against the Christian religion!"

"How so?"

"Why, ye ken ye canna sing the psalms of David without having salvation and such words in four syllables, sal-va-ci-on, and he's making all the children say salvashun."

English spelling doesn't help pronunciation. In fact, it hinders it by its lack of system. English pronunciation is capricious, following few spelling rules. The words *Cough, tough,* and *slough* may look alike, but each is pronounced differently. The *o* in *rove, move,* and *dove* all exasperate the beginner. Scores of other anomalies need not be cited here to make this point: Pronunciation of English is probably the most difficult of any language.

Until Webster came along, spelling-book authors, surprisingly, had ignored or overlooked these problems in pronunciation. Noah revolutionized spellers by devising a simple system of notation. To each distinct vowel sound he gave a number, and this figure, placed above the proper letter in each word, indicated the pronunciation for the reader. For example:

1
name—long a
2
man—short a
3
bald—broad a

The young author followed "general custom," as he put it, or common usage, as we would now express it, as a standard of pronunciation, but this usually meant the New England form. As he traveled more, he heard other pronunciations and gradually culled some of the New England provincialisms out of his later editions. However, most of them remained, and—for better or worse—New England's speech became a general standard for the nation.

In using current speech, rather than some other source of correctness, Webster again showed his gift of prescience. Nearly 150 years later, the National Council of Teachers of English recommended common usage as the standard for correctness.

Thanks largely to Webster's speller, Americans' speech habits are fixed despite the wide geographic diversity of the nation and the un-English background of many of its inhabitants. Until television and radio pervaded the consciousness of the world's people, national unity in written and spoken speech among large nations existed only in America.

At the time of the Revolution, doubt existed that English

would even continue as the national language. Extremists advocated adoption of an utterly different tongue, preferably Greek, although theologians favored Hebrew. Others believed that the American version of English would gradually drift away from British English, as Portuguese has from Spanish and Swedish from Danish. Noah Webster thought this, too. Early in his career, he actually welcomed such a drift, but he came to see its dangers. His eventual position is expressed in a quotation from *The Rambler:* "He that wishes to be counted among the benefactors of posterity must add, by his own toil, to the acquisitions of his ancestors."

Webster found more alarming the possibility that regional dialects would evolve into virtually separate languages in America, thus hampering national unity. In England as late as 1843, the year of Webster's death, a Yorkshireman could not converse with a man from Cornwall. A peasant of the Ligurian Apennines could drive his goats home at evening over hills that look down on six provinces, none of whose dialects he could speak. Not so in the United States. Here, Americans from Maine to Hawaii can readily understand each other. We owe it to Webster.

Now it's hard to realize the localism and pride of locality that existed in Webster's America. Localism even extended to such things as tools. A Connecticut ax handle was deliberately different from a Pennsylvania ax handle in design and ornamentation. Bostonians pronounced *chair, cheer,* and were proud that they didn't make it rhyme with *air* as the Virginians did. A person living in New York thought of himself as a New Yorker, not as an American, in 1783. So many German settlers had already flooded Pennsylvania that the English spoken in some areas proved almost unintelligible to outsiders.

In seeking copyrights for his speller, Webster used the argument that his book was "calculated to extirpate the improprieties and vulgarisms which were necessarily introduced by settlers from various parts of Europe; to reform the abuses and corruption which, to an unhappy degree, tincture the conversation of the polite part of the Americans; to render the acquisition of the language easy both to American youth and foreigners; and especially to render the pronunciation of it accurate and uniform by demolishing those odious distinctions of provincial dialects which are the subject of reciprocal ridicule in different States."

To John Canfield, a Sharon lawyer whose daughter he had taught, Webster wrote: "America must be as independent in *literature* as she is in *politics*—as famous for arts as for arms,—and it is not impossible but a person of my youth may have some influence in exciting a spirit of literary industry."

Indeed, he did influence that industry. A brash young schoolmaster laid the groundwork for a unifying culture that helped America achieve her greatness.

Chapter 5

COPYRIGHT AND THE "AUTHOR'S SOIL"

In preparing his speller, Noah Webster was like a man who can't swim and who suddenly finds himself in deep water. He had better learn to swim quickly if he hopes to survive.

A problem even more demanding than writing the book proved to be securing copyrights for it in all the states. The 24-year-old Webster tackled the challenge in his characteristically direct way, but it proved more difficult in both time and money than he had bargained for. Before he had lined up a printer, he began in 1782 to besiege various state legislatures in person and by letter to grant him a copyright for his book. The following is Noah's first memorial to a legislature. (Later, he added this note to it: "This was too late to get a hearing this session and the work much altered and enlarged. It now appears under the title *Grammatical Institute &c.*")

To THE GENERAL ASSEMBLY OF CONNECTICUT
Hartford, October 24, 1782.

To the honourable the General Assembly of the State of Connecticut, the memorial of Noah Webster, late of Hartford in Connecticut and now of Goshen in Orange County and State of New York, humbly sheweth that your memorialist has with great labor and experience compiled a work which he proposes to call *The American Instructor* to be printed in two volumes; the first volume, being a proper Spelling Book, contains an amendment of those tables and lessons of short easy words in the Spelling

56

Book of Mr. [Thomas] Dilworth which were liable to exception and which are here rendered more plain for children. Instead of the proper names for places which belong to Great Britain, which we are incapable and unwilling to learn and which are totally useless in America, your memorialist has inserted those words only which occur in the sacred or other writings which are of obvious use and difficult pronunciation, together with the names of the Kingdoms of Europe, their capital cities, and the United States of America—the counties, principal towns, and rivers in each seperate [sic] state—with other improvements of obvious utility.

Instead of that long treatise of grammar of Mr. Dilworth, which in the most material points bears not the least analogy to the nature and idioms of the English language, the last volume contains an abridgment of grammar, extracted from the most approved modern writers upon the subject, with his own observations and some notes pointing out the most common and flagrant errors in speaking and writing, the whole being reduced to the capacity of children. In addition to this he has inserted a few easy dialogues calculated to attract the attention of children and which, experience has taught your memorialist, are the best adapted to teach children to read with propriety, and almost the only method to break ill habits in pronunciation; and also some remarks upon the vices of mankind, designed to inspire youth with an abhorrence of vice and love of virtue and religion. To close the whole is annexed a short account of the discovery of America, the time of the settlement of each state, with an epitome of their respective constitutions as established since the revolution—which is designed to diffuse a political knowledge of this grand confederation of republics among that class of people who have not access to more expensive means of information.

Your memorialist, ever ambitious to promote the interest of literature and the honor and dignity of the American empire, designs the above-mentioned work for the general benefit of youth in the United States. And in order to prevent spurious editions and to enable your memorialist to have the book under his own correction, and especially to secure to him the pecuniary advantages of his own productions to which he conceives himself solely entitled, your memorialist therefore humbly prays that this honorable Assembly would appoint a committee to examine into the merit and usefulness of the performance and upon their favorable report would, by a law passed for purposes, vest in your memorialist and his assigns the exclusive right of printing, publishing, and vending the said American Instructor in the State of Connecticut for and during the term of thirteen years from the passing of said act, or for such other term of time as this honorable assembly shall in their wisdom see proper. And your Memorialist, as in duty bound, shall ever pray.

Statutory copyright dates only from the eighteenth century anywhere in the world. England enacted the law first and the

United States second—thanks almost solely to Noah Webster. The earliest French law came into force in 1791. The first American acts —secured as a result of Webster's efforts in Connecticut, Massachusetts, and Maryland—were all passed by 1783. By 1786 all the original 13 states but Delaware had passed copyright laws. Article I, section 8 of the Constitution provides for it. Noah Webster's earlier lobbying in the state legislatures helped make the United States the first nation on earth to provide for copyright in its fundamental law.

Yet this Constitutional provision still needed statutory expression, and this came in the second session of the First Congress, meeting in New York, on May 31, 1790. Granted were rights for 14 years, with an extension for another 14 years. The 14 derived from a multiple of seven under old Royal Patents.

The initial amendment to the law came on January 1, 1803; it added prints to the articles and books already subject to copyright. The new copyright law of February 3, 1831, completely revised the copyright law, increasing the terms from 14 years to 28, with another 28 allowed upon renewal. Those same terms remain to this day. Webster's hand appears in all these state and federal mutations. Late in life he recounted his role in copyright legislation. It is worth setting down here his account because it accurately records the chronology of events, and underplays his part as the father of the American copyright, thus contradicting charges against him of unbridled vanity and outrageous self-advertising. It also demonstrates one of his prose styles—unadorned exposition—that contrasts pleasantly with the purple polemics and bombast that characterize some of his earlier writings.

In October following I went to Hartford, with a view to petition the Legislature of Connecticut, then in session in that place, for a law to secure to me the copyright of my proposed book. The petition was presented, but too late in the session to obtain a hearing. I then returned to Goshen, and devoted the winter to a revision of my manuscripts, and the introduction of some improvements which had been suggested by gentlemen in Princeton and Philadelphia. In January, 1783, I prepared another memorial to be presented to the Legislature of Connecticut, for the purpose of procuring a copyright law, which memorial was committed to the care of John Canfield, Esq. But the necessity of it was superseded by the enactment of a general law upon the subject. This law was obtained by the petition of several literary gentlemen in that State.

In the same winter I went to Kingston, in Ulster County, New York, where the legislature was in session, with a view to present a petition for the like purpose. The necessity of such petition was prevented by the prompt attention of General Schuyler to my request, through whose influence the bill was introduced into the Senate, which at the next session became a law. In the same winter the Legislature of Massachusetts enacted a copyright law, procured probably, by the agency of the Rev. Timothy Dwight, then a member of the House of Representatives.

As Congress, under the Confederation had no power to protect literary property several gentlemen, among them was Joel Barlow, presented a memorial to that body petitioning them to recommend to the several States the enactment of such a law. In May, 1783, on the report of Mr. Williamson, Mr. Izard, and Mr. Madison, Congress passed a resolution, recommending to the several States to secure to authors or publishers of new books for a term not less than fourteen years. In December, 1783, Governor Livingston informed me by letter that the Legislature of New Jersey had passed a law agreeable to the recommendation of Congress.

In May, 1785, I undertook a journey to the Middle and Southern States, one object of which was to procure copyright laws to be enacted. I proceeded to Charleston, but the legislature not being in session, I returned to Baltimore, where I spent the summer. In November I visited General Washington at his mansion; he gave me letters to Governor Harrison in Richmond, and to the speakers of both houses of the legislature. The law desired was passed for securing copyrights. In December I visited Anapolis, where the legislature was in session; and in February I visited Dover, in Delaware, for the same purpose. On petition, the Legislature of Delaware appointed a committee to prepare a bill for a copyright law, just at the close of the session, but the enactment was deferred to the next session. In the year 1790 Congress enacted their first copyright law, which superseded all the state laws on the subject.

When I was in England in 1825, I learned that the British Parliament had, a few years before, enacted a new law on copyrights, by which the rights of authors were much extended. This led me to attempt to procure a new law in the United States, giving a like extension to the rights of authors. My first attempt appears in the following letter [to the Hon. Daniel Webster, dated September 30, 1826]:—

". . . I sincerely desire that while you are a member of the House of Representatives in Congress your talents may be exerted in placing this species of property on the same footing as all property as to exclusive right and permanence of possession.

"Among all modes of acquiring property, or exclusive ownership, the act or operation of creating or making seems to have the first claim. If anything can justly give a man an exclusive right to the occupancy and enjoyment of a thing it must be the fact that he made it. The right of a farmer and mechanic to the exclusive enjoyment and right of disposal of what they make or produce is never questioned. What, then, can make a difference between the produce of muscular strength and the produce of the intellect? If it should be said that as the purchaser of a bushel of wheat has obtained not only the exclusive right to the use of it for food, but the right to sow it and increase and profit by it, let it be replied, this is true; but if he sows the wheat he must sow it on his own ground or soil. The case is different with respect to the copy of a book, which a purchaser has obtained, for the copyright is the author's soil, which the purchaser cannot legally occupy.

"Upon what principles, let me ask, can any fellow-citizens declare that the production of the farmer and the artisan shall be protected by common law, or the principles of natural and social rights, without a special statue, and without paying a premium for the enjoyment of their property, while they declare that I have only a temporary right to the fruits of my labor, and even this cannot be enjoyed without giving a premium? Are such principles as these consistent with the established doctrines of property, and of moral right and wrong among an enlightened people? Are such principles consistent with the high and honorable notions of justice and equal privileges which our citizens claim to entertain and to cherish as characteristic of modern improvements of civil society? How can the recent origin of a particular species of property vary the principles of ownership? I say nothing of the inexpedience of such a policy, as it regards the discouragement of literary exertions. . . .

To this letter Mr. Webster returned the following answer:—

"Boston, October 14, 1826.

"Dear Sir,—I have received yours of the 30th of September, and shall, with your permission, lay it before the committee of the judiciary next session, as that committee has in contemplation some important changes in the law respecting copyright. Your opinion, in the abstract, is certainly right and uncontrovertible. Authorship is, in its nature, ground of property. Most people, I think, are as well satisfied (or better) with the reasoning of Mr. Justice Yates as with that of Lord Mansfield in the great case of Miller and Taylor. But after all, property, in the social state, must be the creature of law; and it is a question of expediency, high and general, not particular expediency, how and how far the rights of authorship should be protected. I confess frankly that I see, or think I see objections to make it perpetual. At the same time I am willing to extend it further than at present, and am fully persuaded that it ought to be relieved from all charges such as depositing copies, etc.

"Yours, D. Webster."

In the autumn of 1827 I applied to the Hon. Mr. Ingersoll, a representative from Connecticut, stating to him the facts of an extension of copyright in Great Britain, as also in France, and requesting him to use his influence to have a bill for a new law brought forward in Congress. . . . [However, a bill and amendment died in committee.]

At the next session (1829–1830) the Hon. Mr. Ellsworth, a member from Connecticut, was appointed one of the judiciary committee, of which the Hon. Mr. Buchanan was chairman. Before Mr. Ellsworth left home, I applied to him to make efforts to procure the enactment of a new copyright law, and sent a petition to Congress, praying for the renewal of the copyright of one of my books. This petition, being referred to the judiciary committee, brought the subject distinctly into consideration. After consultation, the committee authorized Mr. Ellsworth to prepare a bill for a general law on the subject. In order to present the subject in its true light to the committee and to Congress, Mr. Ellsworth wrote notes to the ministers of the principal European nations, requesting information from each of them respecting the state of copyrights in the nations they represented. From their answers and an inspection of the laws of some of the governments, Mr. Ellsworth framed a report, stating the terms of time for which copyrights are secured to authors in Great Britain, France, Russia, Sweden, Denmark and certain states in Germany. He also framed a bill for a law intended to embrace all the material provisions of the old laws with those of the bill reported by the former judiciary committee.

On this bill Mr. Ellsworth introduced some valuable provisions which had been omitted in the old laws, and in the bill and amendment offered at the former session. He also obtained from his friends some suggestions which enabled him to correct some errors and supply defects. This bill was approved by the judiciary committee, reported by Mr. Ellsworth and printed by order of the House. But such was the pressure of business, and so little interest was felt in the bill, that no efforts of Mr. Ellsworth could bring it before the House at that session.

Finding the efforts of the friends of the bill in Congress to be unavailing to obtain a hearing, I determined in the winter of 1830–1831 to visit Washington myself, and endeavor to accomplish the object. Accordingly I took lodgings at the seat of government, where I passed nine or ten weeks; and during this time read a lecture in the Hall of the Representatives, which was well attended, and as my friends informed me had no little effect in promoting the object of obtaining a law for securing copyrights.

The difficulties which had prevented the bill from being brought forward now disappeared. The bill, at the second reading in the House of Representatives, met with some opposition; but it was ably supported by Mr. Ellsworth, Mr. Verplanck and Mr. Huntington. It passed to a third reading by a large majority, and was ordered to be engrossed without opposition. When the bill came before the Senate, it was referred to the judiciary committee. Mr. Rowan, the chairman being absent, the committee requested the Hon. Daniel Webster to take the bill, examine it, and report it if he thought proper; he did so, and under all circumstances deemed it expedient to report it without amendment. On the second reading Mr. Webster made a few explanatory remarks; no other person uttered a word on the subject; and it passed to a third reading by a unaminous vote. On the third reading, the Senate, on motion, dispensed with the reading, and it passed to be engrossed, without debate.

In my journeys to effect this object and in my long attendance in Washington I expended nearly a year of time. Of my expenses in money I have no account but it is a satisfaction to me that a liberal statute for securing to authors the fruit of their labor has been obtained.

At the bicentennial celebration of Noah Webster's birth, *Publisher's Weekly,* the trade publication, noted in its issue of October 20, 1958: "Especially to be remembered by the book trade and by all writers was his [Webster's] determined and successful efforts for an American copyright law which he personally promoted into the statutes of the thirteen original states and thus assured its recognition in the federal constitution and its later extension in federal statutes."

Although the young author had alleged copyright protection, he still suffered many infringements. Robert Ross's *The New American Spelling Book,* published by Thomas and Samuel Green, New Haven, may have been the first in a line of plagiarisms. Ross lifted whole sections, even copying the fables verbatim.

By 1788 Webster was the plaintiff in many suits against infringement, and he was the defendent in cases brought against him by printers concerning alleged violation of contracts. Not until enactment of the federal copyright law in 1790 could he straighten out most of these tangles, usually for small settlements as plaintiff or for dismissal as defendant. His reputation for rigid honesty in his dealings was already becoming established. Yet until his death copyright infringements tormented him. His corresondence is peppered with references to the problem, involving the speller most of the time.

Webster's own contract printers often turned out to be the culprits. William Young, his Philadelphia printer, had revealed to him the crafty deals between Campbell in New York and Patten in Hartford. Young apparently had hoped that the exposure would net him more favorable terms on the next contract with Webster. His action might have succeeded, except that Webster discovered Young himself had issued abridgements in 1788 of the grammar (Part II of the *Grammatical Institute*) solely for the benefit of his own pocket.

Chapter 6

THE TEXTBOOK FLOOD

Authors rushed to the presses after the Revolution to meet the thirst for education with new textbooks. Webster led the parade, both in the total number of copies sold and in the number of titles. He had anticipated the trend, an early example of his lifelong prescience.

While Dilworth and others had combined a speller, grammar, and reader in one book, Webster shrewdly split them into three separate volumes. If a teacher adopted the speller, he would be induced to adopt the other two, also. The Connecticut schoolmaster in addition derived simpler abridgements of the three for the youngest pupils. So by 1790 he had six textbooks on the market. In the nineteenth century he authored revised versions of these plus others, notably a series entitled *Elements of Useful Knowledge*.

Webster's grammar bore a title even more cumbersome than the speller; *A Grammatical Institute of the English language, in three parts: Part II, containing a plain and comprehensive grammar, founded on the true principles and idioms of the language; with an analytical dissertation, in which the various uses of the auxiliary signs are unfolded and explained; and an essay towards investigating the rules of English verse.*

Again published and printed at his own expense by Hudson & Goodwin, it contained 139 pages and first appeared in March 1784. Like the speller, it followed earlier patterns, largely Dilworth's format on grammar in his *New Guide*. Noah Webster also leaned to some extent on Robert Lowth's *A Short Introduction to English Grammar*, published in 1762. But the American differed

63

from both Englishmen in not following their lead in using principles of logic derived from the Latin language.

Dilworth and Lowth were both clergymen, more accustomed
to teaching adults and college-age men than young boys and girls.
Webster, however, had practical experience with youngsters and
knew firsthand the folly of teaching English as if it were Latin to
beginners who barely knew their own tongue, let alone a dead
foreign language. Furthermore, he knew that children almost universally detest grammar. He tried to simplify it as much as possible.
He clarified the perplexing matter of gender, showing that neuter
is a lack of gender and that the matter has less importance in English
than in other languages. He divided verbs into transitive and in-
transitive, instead of the old division into active, passive, and neuter. He gave some order to the chaos of auxiliary verbs, although
he disingenuously confessed to his young readers that he himself
found the subject difficult. He predicted that the subjunctive mode
and some rarely used tenses would head toward obsolescence and
didn't bother much with them.

Even from today's point of view, Webster showed admirable
sanity in his approach to grammar. In his early editions, his contribution lay not so much in new theories as in lopping off the useless
Latinate terminology and in describing, although not prescribing,
actual grammatical usage. As in spelling, he advocated common
speech practices as the standard to be followed. To that end, he
advocated that *you was* be adopted as the correct form when the
subject is singular. Unfortunately, the pedantically minded among
us have never accepted Webster's commonsense proposal.

The grammar at first sold well; the first edition was exhausted
within a year. Others followed. In 1787 Webster altered the book
to respond to criticism concerning some of the definitions, and he
enlarged the section on punctuation.

Noah Webster had grown increasingly fascinated with the
study of linguistics. He happened upon *Diversions of Purley,* by
Horne Tooke, an English political radical and philologist, who
opened his eyes to the need to study Anglo-Saxon and Gothic in
order to understand fully the English language. While this suggestion had value, others did not. For example, Tooke's perfunctory
researches had led him to categorize conjunctions, prepositions,
interjections, and adverbs in a category called "abbreviations,"
deriving these forms etymologically from verbs. In his desire to

prove other grammarians wrong, Webster adopted this and other Tookeian conclusions too hastily. As a result, his grammar became filled with inconsistencies and inaccuracies. Furthermore, he contentiously carried on the battle against the Latinate grammarians in his introduction. As edition followed edition, the grammar grew more controversial and learned, until it outran the abilities of its young readers—and probably of most teachers, too. In any event, Webster charged that many schoolmasters were illiterate men with no instruction in grammar. His ardor for reform had spoiled his judgment. A grammar by Lindley Murray, published in 1795, took the lead. Although it leaned heavily on Noah's work, it eschewed experiment and controversy.

In 1804, in a move that is still unusual among authors, Webster withdrew his book because of what he termed "imperfections," and because it was "immoral to publish what appeared to be false rules and principles." By 1807 he had revised it so completely that it had become a new work, titled *Philosophical and Practical Grammar.* It never caught on, however. Despite its commercial failure, it remains a good book, the first English grammar based upon a painstaking study of usage. Its examples still serve as an excellent source for disputed points of English style.

Noah Webster also experienced mixed success with his reader. Published as Part III of the *Institute,* the first edition appeared in February 1785, printed by a firm headed by his Yale friend Joel Barlow and Elisha Babcock, who also printed a new weekly newspaper in Hartford, *The American Mercury.* The 186-page book had, again, a cumbersome title: *A Grammatic institute of the English language, in three parts; Part III. Containing, the necessary rules of reading and speaking and a variety of essays, dialogues and declamatory pieces, moral, political and entertaining; divided into lessons for the use of children.* It completed Webster's system that he had advocated for the improvement of American elementary education.

The first edition was not notably nationalistic. It started with four easy rules for reading and speaking, brief hints for proper articulation, pausing, accenting, and gesturing: "Grief is expressed by weeping, stamping the feet, lifting the eyes to heaven, etc." "Hope brightens the countenance, arches the eyebrows, gives an eager wishful look, opens the mouth to half a smile and bends the body a little forward."

After these rules came 31 pages of short prose and verse. They included proverbs, aphorisms, and epigrammatic quotes from Addison, Bacon, Dryden, Franklin, Johnson, Pope, Shakespeare, and Swift. Webster followed these with sentimental tales lifted from other publications, then three original characterizations that he had written, one of which probably described an idealized Juliana Smith of Sharon:

Juliana is one of those rare women whose personal attractions have no rivals, but the sweetness of her temper and the delicacy of her sentiments. An elegant person, regular features, a fine complexion, a lively, expressive countenance, an easy address, and those blushes of modesty that soften the soul of the beholder; These are the native beauties, which render her the object of universal admiration.

But when we converse with her, and hear the melting expression of unaffected sensibility and virtue that flow from her tongue, her personal charms receive new lustre, and irresistibly engage the affections of her acquantance.

Sensible that the great source of all happiness is purity of morals and an easy conscience, Juliana pays constant and sincere attention to the duties of religion. She abhors the infamous, but fashionable device of deriding the sacred institutions of religion.

She considers a lady without virtue as a monster on earth; and every accomplishment, without morals, as polite deception. She is neither a hypocrite nor an enthusiast; on the contrary, she mingles such cheerfulness with the religious duties of life, that even her piety carries with it a charm which insensibly allures the proligate from the arms of vice . . .

Before reading any Freudian undertones into the foregoing, remember that such compositions were typical of the late eighteenth century.

Sterner stuff followed this gossamer writing—selections from the unpublished epics of Barlow and Dwight, a part of Trumbull's *M'Fingal* and a number of dramatic scenes from Shakespeare, Sheridan, and others. Extracts from Congressional speeches, Tom Paine's *Crisis,* and Thomas Days' letter on Negro slavery concluded the volume. Webster showed courage by including this last selection in a book he hoped to sell in the South, although, at this time, even an occasional New Englander owned slaves.

Webster used the reading of dialogue as a teaching device. In his preface he wrote: "It is found by experience that dialogues, as bearing a near resemblance to the common talk of children, are the best calculated to prevent or break the ill habits of reading, and to teach them an easy unaffected pronunciation."

Although the edition of 1785 carried a minimum amount of patriotic material, Webster issued a new reader in 1787 that had twice as many pages (372) as the first version and carried a new title as a sign of its altered purpose: *An American selection of lessons in reading and speaking. Calculated to improve the minds and refine the taste of youth. And also to instruct them in geography, history and politics of the United States. To which is prefixed, rules in elocution, and directions for expressing the principal passions of the mind.*

Patriotism burst from the pages because Webster thought its fires needed to be rekindled. He prepared the new edition while in Philadelphia during the deliberations of the Constitutional Convention. If the Revolution stirred him, the Convention and the new Constitution set him afire with nationalistic zeal. We'll see later some of the other results of his ardor, but his new reader was one of the first.

The new edition leaned heavily on selections from the writings and addresses of the founders of the republic—Warren's and Hancock's orations on the Boston Massacre, Congressional speeches, the Declaration of Independence, Washington's Farewell Orders to the army and circular letter. Webster wrote more than 50 pages of new material for the book. He recorded the histories of the discovery of North America and of the Revolutionary War. This was the first textbook in the United States to give a history of the nation's formation. Another departure was a brief geography of the United States, but he later dropped this when fellow Yale graduate, Jedidiah Morse, wrote a school geography that was almost universally adopted by 1795.

Webster also included in *An American Selection* his lecture, "Remarks on the manners, government, laws, and domestic debt of America," which strongly argued for national manners and a national language. He took to the nationalistic route deliberately, hoping to start patriotism early among youth.

Perhaps Webster succeeded in this for a time, but his book had lost first place to others by 1800, notably to Caleb Bingham's *American Preceptor,* first published in 1794. However, the Webster book was reprinted as late as 1816. Webster reissued it with changes in 1835 "to instruct our youth in what belongs to this country." Although a somewhat testy curmudgeon by then, he still loved his nation.

Noah Webster was again first, this time with the reader. He began the long trend of American readers, including the famous McGuffey series. His little book was the precursor of the modern graded readers, although his were not actually graded.

Between 1786 and 1790 Webster prepared abridgments of his speller, grammar, and reader for the youngest children. The first was his edition of *The New England Primer,* an old standby since 1690. Although he retained the name, he changed everything else, softening the harsh Calvinistic tone of the original. For the old illustration of the first letter in the alphabet—

> In Adam's Fall
> We Sinned all,

he offered:

> A was an apple-pie made by the cook.

Little stories taught the morals that Juliana Smith had ridiculed. A boy went into the water and nearly drowned. When rescued, "he said he was sorry he had not minded his parents."

The second little book was an abridgement of the grammar that he called *An introduction to English grammar.* An innovation was "A Federal Catechism," the first simple explanation, for use in schools, of the new Constitution and of how our government worked.

Later in 1790 Webster compiled *The Little Reader's Assistant.* This included the rudiments of reading and speaking plus 21 short tales explaining incidents from American life and history or illustrating humanitarian motives. He included two antislavery narratives.

With these six little books written between 1783 and 1790, Webster piled up an impressive list of firsts:

1. First to prepare a system of education.
2. First to give rules of versification to children.
3. First to see the need for and to do something about securing copyright laws.

4. First to publish selections from budding American writers.
5. First to write and teach American history and civics.
6. First to foster a consciousness of nationality.
7. First to insist upon nationality in language, manners, and education.
8. First to prepare books to teach children these principles.
9. First to foster America's feeling of democratic idealism.

By his example, Webster opened the way for a flood of textbooks —most of them with the word "American" in their titles—by many writers. He helped his fellow authors in another way too, for he was the first to show them how to sell books to their fellow Americans.

Chapter 7

THE YANKEE PEDDLER

Noah Webster's speller was the first successful book published in the United States, another and very important first. Such an accomplishment didn't just happen, however. Noah showed himself worthy of today's most persevering book-club strategists. In the eighteenth century, Americans weren't book buyers in the way that they are today. Only the wealthy and educated citizens bought books, most of them books imported from England. Libraries were few in number, and most libraries had small, partially obsolete collections.

The Connecticut schoolmaster had to resort to ingenious methods to sell his speller, whose sales eventually reached a conservatively estimated 100 million copies. He tried a multifaceted approach. First, Webster turned his copyright efforts into an advertising campaign by widely publicizing his memorials to the various legislators. Second, he advertised his books in newspapers. When he became the editor of a Federalist newspaper, he ran in it constant advertisements and announcements of new editions of the speller. Country merchants began to lay in supplies when they came to the nearest trading town as confidently as they bought West India goods or English tools.

Third, Webster persuaded others to promote his books. A typical letter to Hudson & Goodwin in 1788 says:

When you advertise the improved editions of the *Institute,* the author has taken great pains to examine the subject of language with accuracy and to hear the opinions of the most learned men in every part of America. These advantages have enabled him to correct many errors and supply many defects, which were in the first editions; and he flatters himself the work has attained as great a degree of accuracy as can be given it in the present stage of the language. He hopes that the teachers of schools will not complain of the late alterations; they were necessary and will be useful. Every thing approaches perfection by slow degrees—it is the fate of all human production—but the author intends that all future editions shall be uniform.

It may be useful to notify the public that it is the wish of many leading men in America that all the children in the different states should learn the language in the same book that all may speak alike. The Philological Society in New York recommend this work with a view to make it the Federal school book. The University of Georgia, preferring this to Dilworth, Perry, Fenning, or any other, have determined that this alone shall be used in all the schools in that state. The publishers flatter themselves that the northern states will heartily concur in the design of a *federal language.*

The Philological Society was a typical Websterian promotional body, organized by the author. Nearly its only activity was to endorse his books.

Fourth, Webster donated his books to worthy institutions and publicized his act. On a trip to Charleston, South Carolina, he gave 200 copies of the speller and 100 of the grammar to the Mt. Zion Society, sponsors of Winnsborough College. In a letter of appreciation, the society's secretary assured Webster that "the production of a native of America at so early a period after her arduous and successful struggle for freedom and independence, must reflect the highest honour on the ability and liberality of the author." Local newspapers ran an equally flowery tribute. Campbell, the New York printer who had South Carolina as part of his franchise, protested the author's generosity, but it was a master stroke that made both the speller and grammar standard in the state. As another gesture of generosity and goodwill, Noah gave his Connecticut royalties to a scholarship for some worthy student at Yale, but his conditions ruled that a recipient could be neither a duelist nor a seducer.

Fifth, Webster deposited his books for sale with the postmaster (who was often the local tavern keeper in those days) and with the local printer, as well as with general storekeepers. He anticipated by more than a century today's paperback sales outlets.

Sixth, he lectured on a variety of subjects—usually language or American nationalism—and he used the opportunity for a none too subtle plug for his books. Newspaper accounts usually identified Webster as "the author of . . ." (naming a particular book), because he took the trouble to visit the newspaper editor. If necessary Webster even wrote the article himself under a pseudonym.

Seventh, he showed a propensity for getting into controversies concerning his books that generated publicity. An example relates to the so-called "Dilworth's Ghost." A Litchfield schoolmaster named Hughes grumbled in 1784 at the upstart who displaced the tried and true Dilworth. When the second edition of Webster's speller appeared in June 1784, Hughes anonymously sent a long, punning denunciatory letter to the *The Freeman's Chronicle* (a publication only recently established in Hartford by Noah's cousin, Bavil Webster), signing it "Dilworth's Ghost." The "Ghost" criticized Webster for plagiarism, poor judgment, an "inelegant and bombastick" style, inconsistency, vicious pronunciation, and spleen, ambition, avarice, arrogance, and lack of candor. Finally, he sneered at Webster's copyright effort as "truly a very laughable affair."

Such an attack might have crushed most young men not yet 26 years old. Not Webster. He wrote an adroit reply that didn't answer a single criticism, but suggested that he would respond fully only to signed and grammatically correct complaints. In effect, he wished to prolong the debate. When the "Ghost" didn't rise to the challenge, despite the fact that the original "Ghost" article had been copied by other papers, Webster prepared a detailed reply in which he defended himself on all counts. His comments on his style belie the charges of vanity that he increasingly heard: "If this be too plain and pointed, it must be ascribed to the feeling of a man, who, after he had spent years in the study of language, found that he was totally unacquainted with the elements of his own; that he had been learning errors himself and teaching them to others. . . . But so blind was my respect and veneration . . . that in the first edition I adopted many things as right, which I since find to be wrong."

That seemed to be that, but later "A Learner of English Grammar" complained about Webster's pronunciation. "Ghost" and somebody calling himself "Entity" took up pens, and a roaring debate in the press lasted for months. One of Webster's anonymous critics accused him of trying to suppress the opposition. Webster disingenuously rebutted: "I am under ten thousand obligations . . . for [the Ghost's] spiteful attempt to depreciate my publications. Had not his scurrilous remarks appeared, people would have taken less pains to examine the design, the plan, and the merit of the *Institute*. The result of a critical examination into the work has generally been in its favour."

In fact the quarrel netted Noah a printer in Boston, Benjamin Edes. Booksellers throughout the new nation laid in supplies. If the uproar did not make him a celebrity, it did make him an object of curiosity, and it definitely increased the sale of his books.

Yet Webster did more in these controversies than merely try to promote sales. He chose these occasions to promote his ideas on education, language, and nationalism. However, he had a coy way about him that could irritate and prolong a discussion, as seen in this passage from a letter to "Dilworth's Ghost" in January 1785: "What alterations I have made in our system of education appear to be built on firm principles; but if this should not be the case, their weakness will be easily detected and the neglect of my publication will be considered as a fortunate event by the Public's most humble Servant, Noah Webster, Jun."

As this and other statements illustrate, he had an unwitting gift of alienating his best supporters, antagonizing political or sectional groups, and rubbing audiences the wrong way.

In the introduction to his speller's 1783 edition he wrote: "The criticisms of those who know more, will be received with gratitude; the censure or ridicule of those who know less will be inexcusable." Although he softened this wording in later editions, his remark accurately expresses how he felt about critics for the rest of his life. No wonder he generated controversy!

The dissensions alarmed his family. Noah's father wrote in a letter of July 28, 1787: "I have had a hint son from some gentlemen and some newspapers as though you have made some unfriendly to you by some of your writings and done your self damage. I would caution you to be wise as a serpent as well as harmless as a dove. Have courage but temper the same with prudence."

The "Ghost" dispute also revealed Webster's sarcastic side. To a challenge to his scholarship in the *Institute* he replied: "You have heard also, Mr. Ghost, that I was once a *poor school master* worth nothing. This is true, and a very substantial proof that my grammar is good for nothing. A *poor* man must produce a *poor* book; that is certain."

Eighth, Webster solicited aid from influential people. Despite —or perhaps because of—his aggressiveness, Webster enjoyed surprising success at this, getting testimonials by the hundreds, particularly from older men. Nor did rebuffs seem to discourage him. Although Washington and Franklin refused to endorse his speller, Webster continued to court them, and for the most part he was successful. To that end, he may have allowed himself to be persuaded to further certain of Franklin's ideas for spelling reforms. Although the young schoolmaster adopted some of these reforms, he knew too much about language and human nature to accept all.

Webster's patrons helped in other ways, too. Benjamin Franklin made professional observations on the quality of the printing. "Your Spelling Book is miserably printed here," he told Webster, "so as in many places to be scarcely legible, and on wretched paper."

But Noah knew when not to go too far. Campbell and Young in 1788 used a portrait of Washington as a frontispiece. Webster was chagrined. "It is using the General disrespectfully to make him a passport for spelling books," he protested. However, many of his editions carried long lists of the names of worthies who endorsed the book.

Webster frequently introduced new editions of his most successful books to stimulate sales and to foil the widespread piracy. The long life of some of his volumes also necessitated new editions to keep up with the times.

Finally, ninth, Webster traveled tirelessly to promote his books, mainly the speller. In this he copied the techniques of the Yankee peddlers, or traveling salesmen of the late eighteenth and early nineteenth centuries. Until about 1810, these merchants were usually known as chapmen or petty chapmen. The term Yankee peddler had not yet come into use, although Yankees were increasingly the chapmen of the time. They eventually so dominated the trade that the term chapman fell into disuse and was gradually replaced by Yankee peddler.

Even in his 84th year, the last year of his life, Webster still made his annual Yankee peddler trips, combining business with visits to his daughters.

Noah made his journeys serve two purposes, to secure copyrights and to promote sales. In May 1785, he began a long trip—mostly on horseback, but varied by boat and coaching stage. Often, he noted in his diary, the roads were terrible. An entry for May 18, 1785 reads: "Set out for Alexandria; stage wagon breaks down—I curse all stage wagons and return to town—loiter about and do little, but hire a horse."

Wherever the author went, he showed the rough draft of his book. He approached anyone of prominence. On his way to Richmond, Virginia, in November 1785, he stopped at General Washington's home at Mount Vernon and passed the night entertaining the general's family and friends with his discussions about the new nation and language. This meeting confirmed him in his devotion to Washington and to his policies and had a strong effect on his later political sympathies.

Webster sought the support of humbler men, too. He rode horseback from village to village, seeing preachers, teachers, lawyers, and school committees. He gave copies of his speller to printers with the request: "Hereafter spell according to this book."

Noah kept up this tireless spadework, not for just a few years, but for the rest of his life. He early saw the book-buying potential of the opening West and sent his hapless son, William, to Cincinnati and later Lafayette, Indiana, to exploit the opportunity.

The speller took on a life of its own. Emigrant preachers and teachers carried it West. Editions were printed without Webster's permission or knowledge. As each settlement sprang up, the speller laid the foundation of education and contributed to national unity. In the 1840s an edition of the speller came out in the Oregon Territory.

No detail concerning the commercial life of his speller was too trivial for Webster's attention. His unpublished letters bristle with questions to printers about sales figures, queries about how the book was moving, and suggestions on how to spur sales of his product.

Yet Webster's ethical sense never deserted him, despite his desire for high volume. He sometimes chided his son, William, for hyperbole in the ads he wrote for the speller. And he carefully rebutted his old tutor, Joseph Buckminster, when that clergyman wrote asking if he were not too severe in his criticism of Dilworth. To modern readers, Webster's treatment of Dilworth and Lowth does sound harsh, but it was common practice in the eighteenth century to ridicule the opposition. Noah never went too far in personal criticism, which his contemporaries commonly resorted to. He charged his opponents with faulty grammatical theory—and he was right.

For all his success with the speller and other books, Webster remained dissatisfied. On several birthdays during the 1780s he entered some morose comments in the diary he had begun in 1784: "30 years of my life gone—a large portion of the ordinary age of man! I have read much, and tried to do much good, but with little advantage to myself."

Noah Webster remained a man in search of a mission. Writing school books for children consumed only a part of his enormous energies. He turned again to public issues. In late 1783 he added to his original four articles on "Observations on the Revolution of America" with two more that criticized the concept of established religion and argued "that the purity of the religion and the peace of society depend on giving an unlimited indulgence to all sectaries." The two articles appeared in *The Freeman's Chronicle.*

At the next session, the state legislature passed a toleration act granting each Connecticut citizen the right to prove his affiliation with a nonestablished church, thus escaping the payment of rates to the Congregational Church. Webster, the propagandist, was learning the art of timing. His papers appeared at the ideal moment to influence the legislature.

In this same period, he entered two other, related disputes. One involved paying for the cost of war. Particularly upsetting to thrifty Yankees was a grant of five years' full pay to officers of the American Army, which was intended to indemnify losses that they had sustained while receiving pay in depreciated currency.

Nonofficers and civilians claimed that they too had suffered losses from depreciation, and the whole issue broadened into a widespread discontent about taxation in general.

Writing under the pseudonym "Honorius" in *The Connecticut Courant,* beginning in August 1783, Webster dealt with what he rightly considered a more fundamental question, how the various states could pay their bills under a more equitable system of taxation. He proposed that the national Congress levy a national impost upon imported articles and that this income go for the payment of interest and principal on bonds issued to cover the entire war debt. This action would pool the states' debts and remove the inequalities created by the fact that such states as Connecticut, New Jersey, and North Carolina had little direct international trade. In those days, the biggest source of public income came from tariffs on imports, or imposts. The trouble arose because some states that didn't import much from abroad looked to their neighboring states as sources for tariff income, just as though they were foreign nations. This of course threatened national unity. For the first time, the schoolmaster began thinking about the need for a stronger central government.

Although Webster's pleas for unity had not persuaded all Americans to forgo their factional disputes, they persuaded enough Connecticut voters who, in the next election, voted into the state legislature a slate of legislators favorable to paying the army officers' pensions and to empowering the national legislature to levy a national impost.

Connecticut Governor John Trumbull thanked Webster in person for his efforts, and a state legislator, Stephen Mix Mitchell, said that Webster had "done more to allay popular discontent and support the authority of Congress at this crisis than any other man."

Unfortunately, the publicist Webster didn't please everyone. Among his sensible suggestions he inserted comments such as: "The inhabitants of New England have the character of being knaves and hypocrites." He criticized his opponents' "vile, impolitic manners" and charged that they were a "nest of vipers, disturbing the tranquility of government to answer selfish purposes." He even went so far as to claim that "every attempt to keep alive the present jealousies, to foment divisions and create new animosities, must be treason against the state."

Although Webster wrote under pseudonyms, his identity surfaced. Spying on mail had reached such notorious levels that public figures frequently wrote in cypher or avoided the public mail altogether and had their correspondence hand-delivered by someone trustworthy.

One critic called Webster "a sneaky, snaky, fainthearted

Whig," and another charged that his "dirty squibs will avail . . . no more than spitting against the north wind."

It's likely that his political opponents began attacking his books as a means of retribution. Some may have joined in the "Dilworth's Ghost" uproar as a way of paying him back on the impost and pension controversies, which ran concurrently.

By 1784 Webster had succeeded in getting his name before the public as an author of textbooks and as a political writer. His diary reveals his peripatetic activities. He moved his Hartford residence several times and began reviewing law again. He enjoyed social activities and the ladies, although he claimed "my heart is my own." He listed the eligible girls in the town, but philosophized in an entry for April 4, 1784: "At home. Read a little, had some company, and visited the Ladies in the evening as usual. If there were but one pretty Girl in town, a man could make a choice—but among so many! one's heart is pulled twenty ways at once. The greatest difficulty, however, is that after a man has made *his* choice, it remains the lady to make *hers*".

Earlier, he had been sick and had made this sententious comment in his diary:

March 13th [1784]. At home very unwell. The little indispositions of life are essential to happiness. Uninterrupted felicity never fails to cloy; indeed there is very little pleasure without preceding pain. The author of the universe seems to have framed it with a view to give his creatures an opportunity to exert virtues, which could not exist without natural and moral evil. If it were impossible for mankind to sin, there would be no virtue in preserving their rectitude. If there were no pain, misery, misfortune, or danger to which they could be exposed, patience, humanity, fortitude and prudence would be empty names. The result of this doctrine is to teach us a peaceable submission to the evils of life and calm acquiescence in the disposition of the devine providence which suffers no more evils to take place in the system than are necessary to produce the greatest possible good.

His diary contains numerous comments—both favorable and unfavorable—on Calvinistic sermons he had heard. Although he disapproved of an established church in theory and expressed intellectual dissatisfaction with the church of his fathers, in practice he remained faithful to the Congregationalism of his youth. Furthermore, Webster enjoyed singing in the choir. He evidently had a better than average voice. Even near the end of his life he still sang "in a very true quavering voice," according to a grandaughter.

Noah also continued to play the flute. A 1784 diary entry notes: "Musing myself with books and with a flute. What an infinite variety of methods have [sic] man invented to render life agreeable! What a wise and happy design in the human frame that the sound of a little hollow tube of wood should dispel in a few moments, or at least alleviate, the heaviest cares of life."

His "heaviest cares" may have been his languishing law practice. He opened an office in the summer of 1784, but few clients came to him. He did win his first courtroom victory in pleading the case of someone named Bidwell against Abiel Wilson. The judge at the trial was Noah's father sitting as a justice of the peace. Young Webster had few notable cases; most involved debt, the usual cause for litigation in that era. In one Connecticut county court appeared 1,100 actions in one year, 95 percent of them for debts of only five or six pounds.

So, the young lawyer had plenty of time to attend to his textbooks and his newspaper articles. He did get one important case, but more because of his skills as a publicist than as a lawyer. Connecticut had laid claim to land along the north branch of the Susquehanna River at Wyoming, within the present borders of Pennsylvania. In 1784 Pennsylvania disputed Connecticut's claim and drove the newcomers out with military force. Congress was too weak to settle the matter and the issue of ownership remained unresolved. A group of Connecticut men, including Noah Webster, Sr., had earlier formed a stock company to develop the area. They hired Noah, Jr., to represent them and to publicize their cause. He did so in a series of seven articles published concurrently in the *Courant* and *The American Mercury,* beginning January 3, 1785. He sketched the history of the grants, the events in the controversy, and the larger problem of disposing of the western lands, such as the land involved in this dispute. While Webster's clients wanted their rights recognized or their investments returned, young Noah saw the broader issue. He foresaw possible civil war if each state rushed to claim new lands within the limits of overlapping, ill-defined colonial grants. His solution was: Apportion the western lands among the states and use the proceeds from the sale or rental of these lands to pay the state and national debts.

He suggested, alternatively, that all states cede their claims to unallocated or disputed lands to the United States for the common benefit of all. (Virginia and New York had already offered to do this, or had actually done so.)

While there was no clearcut victory in the case for Webster's clients, its importance to him lies in the fact that it nudged him even closer to what for a time he saw as his mission in life—to be an advocate for patriotism and nationalism.

PART THREE

Webster the Patriot

Chapter 8

THE ROUTE TO UNION

If Americans of the late twentieth century are concerned at what seems to be the crumbling of the national governmental institutions, consider the Americans of the period from 1783 to 1789. They had no such institutions at all.

Webster called the national government under the Articles of Confederation "a ridiculous farce, a burlesque on government." But he wasn't the first to call for stronger central powers than those provided under the confederation.

In 1780 Alexander Hamilton pointed out the defects of excessive state sovereignty, and a year later he wrote "The Continentalist," advocating more power for the Congress. In May 1781, Pelatiah Webster, Noah's distant kinsman, publicly urged calling a Continental Convention to write a new constitution. Even state legislatures, which had earlier feared losses of power and had supported the weak plan for confederacy, began to grow restive. In the summer of 1782, the New York Legislature passed a resolution saying that the confederation was defective and that a general convention should be called to remedy it.

Using this state resolution as an argument, Hamilton told Congress on April 1, 1783, that it should authorize such a convention. Earlier, in February 1783, Pelatiah Webster called for a stronger, bicameral Congress in a pamphlet entitled *A Dissertation on the Political Union and the Constitution of the Thirteen United States of North-America: Which is necessary to their Preservation and Happiness.* General Washington, a cautious man, even entered the discussion in his Circular Address to the Governors of the states on June 1783, stressing the need for "a supreme power to regulate and govern the general concern of the Confederate Republic."

The weakness and inefficiency of the Congress under the confederation had become notorious. A man elected to it might arrive at the meeting place on the appointed day and find a dozen or more delegates like himself ready for business. But the Articles of Confederation required that each state be represented by at least two delegates and that the representative of at least seven states be present to make a quorum. Unless more than seven states were represented, every decision had to be unanimous; and the assent of nine states was necessary in most matters concerning war, peace, and the appropriation of money.

The first arrivals often had to wait weeks before a quorum assembled. Even when a session organized itself, its continuation remained perilous because, if a member fell sick, attendance might fall below the minimum necessary, and the remaining delegates would then have to wait until the sick grew well or the state sent a substitute.

Each delegate was elected for a one-year term and was prohibited from serving for more than three years in six. So, Congressional membership shifted constantly. Another handicap lay in the Articles' failure to provide a regular executive department. Congress exercised executive powers through special commissions and committees and by appointing three secretaries to manage crucial executive matters—war, finance, and foreign affairs. These three offices often fell vacant, with no new appointment for months.

Even when Congress could muster a quorum, it had no permanent home. A Philadelphia barracks mutiny frightened it from that city in 1783. Thereafter, the delegates wandered from Princeton to Annapolis to Trenton to New York.

Oliver Ellsworth, Noah's lawyer friend and a congressman from Connecticut, commented: "It will soon be of very little consequence where Congress go, if they are not made respectable as well as responsible, which can never be done without giving them a power to perform engagements as well as make them."

Through Ellsworth, other friends, and his own omnivorous reading, Webster kept abreast of the situation. In March 1784, he demanded "a federal head, vested with powers sufficient to compel any particular State to comply with the measures that are adopted by the majority of the States."

As the months followed, his ideas crystallized. He saw that he could do for the nation what he had already done for Connecticut —teach the citizens their duty and secure mass action by popular demand. Furthermore, he saw how his ideas for a national government dovetailed with those for education and language to forge a stronger national identity. He decided to take an eighteenth-century version of a barnstorming tour throughout the new nation to sell his ideas—and, not so incidentally, his books as well.

First, he wrote his opinions on government in February 1785, and published them on March 9, 1785 in a 48-page pamphlet, *Sketches of American Policy. Under the following heads: I. Theory of Government. II. Governments on the Eastern Continent. III. American States; or the principles of the American Constitutions contrasted with those of European States. IV. Plan of Policy for improving the Advantages and perpetuating the Union of the American States.* In this he again leaned heavily on Rousseau.

The first part of the pamphlet, "Theory of Government," concluded that "a representative democracy seems . . . to be the most perfect system that is practicable on earth." The second sketch analyzed the governments of Europe. Webster did this to forestall proponents of the argument that everything has been tried before and nothing works well. In the third sketch he developed the thesis that the American states represent something new in history, "unlike the infant situation of all other nations," and have the added advantage of existing "in the most enlightened period of the world" with "the science and experience of all nations to direct them in forming plans of government." He added that "the American states are superior to all nations" in the institution of schools. And where schools flourish so does liberty, because "it is scarcely possible" for an enlightened people to succumb to tyranny.

In his later disillusionment, he repudiated many of those ideas, but never those of his last sketch which outlined "new principles in modeling" a union of the 13 states along the lines of the state governments. He repeated his earlier statement that "there must be a supreme powere at the head of the union, vested with authority to make laws that respect the states in general and to compel obedience to those laws." He urged the election of a president and a

Congress to represent and govern the 13 states, the power to reside in Congress so that no individual state could control or defeat legislation the way Rhode Island had, when she refused to collect a national impost. The core of Webster's proposal is:

Let Congress be empowered to call forth the force of the continent, if necessary, to carry into effect those measures which they have a right to frame. Let the president, be, *ex officio,* supreme magistrate clothed with authority to execute the laws of the states. Let the superintendent of finance have the power of receiving the public monies and issuing warrants for collection, in the manner the treasurer has, in Connecticut. Let every executive officer have power to enforce the laws, which fall within his province. At the same time, let them be accountable for their administration. Let penalties be annexed to every species of maladministration and exacted with such rigour as is due to justice and public safety. In short, let the whole system of legislation, be the peculiar right of the delegates in Congress, who are always under the control of the people; and let the whole administration be vested in magistrates as few as possible in number and subject to the control of Congress only. Let every precaution be used in framing laws, but let no part of the subjects be able to resist the execution. Let the people keep, and *forever keep,* the sole right of legislation in their own representatives; but divest themselves wholly of any right to the administration. Let every state reserve its sovereign right of directing its own internal affairs of the continent. Such a plan of government is practicable; and I believe, the only plan that will preserve the faith, the dignity and the union of these American states.

Along with many of his thoughtful contemporaries, Webster feared that the confederation would break up into 13 petty republics or, perhaps worse, become a monarchy. During the uproar over military pensions, some of the former army leaders had advocated just that. Joel Barlow, Webster's friend and Yale classmate, had flirted with the idea and had gone to Boston as an agent from Connecticut to formulate plans for action. *Sketches of American Policy* had persuaded Barlow of the worth of democratic ideals. Ironically, Barlow remained persuaded for the rest of his life while Webster later had strong doubts.

At that time, however, a Rousseauan fervor sustained the young schoolmaster and textbook author. In his last pages, Webster urged several other reforms to strengthen the union: universal education; the end of local prejudices, particularly the hostility already surfacing between the North and the South; the end of interstate taxation; abolition of slavery; uniformity in state constitutions; permission for clergymen to hold elective office; and the end of servile imitation of the manners, the language, and the vices of foreigners.

He ended with a plea for national unity:

We ought to generalize our ideas and our measures. We ought not to consider ourselves as inhabitants of a single state only; but as Americans; as the common subjects of a great empire. We cannot and ought not to divest ourselves of provincial attachments, but we should subordinate them to the general interest of the continent; . . . as a citizen of the American empire, [an individual] has a national interest far superior to all others.

He argued for the need to allow institutions to evolve, and therefore urged that there be machinery to change the Constitution as conditions changed, because "government originates in necessity, and takes its form from the genius and habits of the people."

For the rest of his life, Webster attempted to establish that this fourth sketch was the first written proposal for a structure of government approximating that actually formed by the Constitutional Convention. While many of his contemporaries pooh-poohed the claim as another proof of his vanity, James Kent, the famous American jurist and Constitutional authority, supported him. If Webster had never written the speller or the dictionaries, he would have been awarded a modest place as a figure in the founding of the Republic.

For Noah Webster did more than write about the need for a new Constitution; he traveled throughout the states lecturing, to an extent that no other American did, as to its necessity. He differed significantly from Pelatiah Webster and Hamilton. His kinsman wanted a "chamber of commerce" set up as a court of last resort in matters pertaining to commerce; Hamilton urged merely that Congress's authority be strengthened to include powers of taxation, of disposing of the ungranted land, and of regulating trade. They both pleaded for reforms because of the economic chaos.

Noah took the road of the political philosopher, defining more clearly than anyone else the American democratic ideal. Furthermore, he proposed a practical program to achieve this ideal.

During a period of public apathy in 1785 and 1786, he carried and read his pamphlet from Charleston, South Carolina, to Portsmouth, New Hampshire. It was reprinted in whole or in part in newspapers in Charleston, Baltimore, Philadelphia, and New York. He personally gave a copy to George Washington, who handed it on to James Madison. Madison, that prime mover of the Annapolis Convention and self-elected recording secretary of the Constitutional Convention, mentioned it in the preface of his *Debates* as one of the earliest statements he had seen.

During the 1780s America faced numerous difficulties as a fledgling nation. First, little or no help was forthcoming from abroad, as it had been during the Revolution, because Europe was looking inward to her own problems.

The general British attitude toward the United States just after the Revolution was one of embarrassment. The British just did not want to be reminded of a mistake. In France, then the most populous nation in Europe, the attitude was one of tolerant curiosity. But nobody wanted to trade much with America because the states had not yet paid their debts.

Europe was wary of America for political reasons as well. This was not a period of widespread social or political reform. Absolute monarchies still reigned. The prevalent European view was that Americans were experimenting with some dangerous concepts.

The French charge d'affaires, Monsieur Otto, reported to Versailles his impressions that it would be impossible to unite under one head all the members of the confederation. "Their political interests, their commercial views, their customs and their laws," he wrote, "are so varied that there is not a resolution of Congress which can be equally useful and popular in the South and the North of the Continent. Their jealousy seems an insurmountable obstacle. The inhabitants of the North are fishers and sailors; those of the Central States, farmers; those of the South, planters." Of Connecticut, he wrote: "The people of this state generally have a national character not commonly found in other parts of the country. They come nearer to republican simplicity; without being rich they are all in easy circumstances."

Travelers, mostly French, flocked to America. The best known was Jean de Crevecoeur who gave a romantic picture of the new nation—noble savages and honest, openhearted citizens innocent of the corruption endemic to Europe. More realistic visitors may have been shocked by the reality—the harshness of the land, something the romantics failed to mention. Instead of the rill and zephyr they met with an uneven and often violent climate, extremely bad roads or none at all, except for forest trails, swollen, unbridged rivers, and everywhere the ugly tree stumps which the Americans ignored or saw as a symbol of their conquest of the wilderness.

The country had storms of lightning and thunder unequaled in Europe. In the winter, snows could fall for days on end. In the summer, violent transitions from heat to cold surprised an English traveler who complained "of the N.W. wind, which in this country is the most keen and severe of any that is to be met with on the face of the globe. The wind is perfectly *dry,* and so uncommonly penetrating that I am convinced it would destroy all the plagues of Egypt."

The forest was man's enemy in America. "Compared with France," wrote one traveler, "the entire country is one vast wood." Isaac Weld, a visiting Englishman, wrote of the Americans' "unconquerable aversion to trees." The ground, he said, could not be tilled nor the inhabitants support themselves until the trees were destroyed. "The man that can cut down the largest number, and have the field about his house most clear of them, is looked upon as the most industrious citizen, and the one that is making the greatest improvement in the country. . . ."

Thomas Cooper, a highly educated scientist and theologian who emigrated to Pennsylvania, advised the prospective emigrant to avoid the seven-month winters of New Hampshire and Massachusetts, also the parching summers of New Jersey and the Carolinas. In New Jersey, Cooper reported, you found insects, reptiles, oppressive heat, fevers, and ague. "The influence of a hot sun upon the moist and low land of the American coast almost infallibly subjects an European . . . to attacks of intermittents."

Many visitors commented on the drinking habits of Americans. When drunk, they tended to fight. Indeed, fighting was looked upon as a sport.

French visitors viewed America and its people more leniently. In Connecticut, the Chevalier de Chastellux told of a squirrel hunt. The animals, he wrote, were larger than those in Europe, with thicker fur, and very adroit in leaping from tree to tree. Should a squirrel be wounded without falling, the inconvenience was slight because somebody usually was within hailing distance to cut down the tree. "As squirrels are not rare," observed Chastellux, "one may conclude, and quite rightly, that trees are very common."

Squirrel ragout was tasty and gamy. Travelers frequently carried their food with them. Frenchmen complained frequently of the American bread. Everyone drank coffee and tea. Americans breakfasted on "relishes"—salt fish, beefsteaks, broiled fowls, ham, and bacon. Oysters were much eaten and the shad an excellent fish. "A fanatical law, passed by Quakers," prohibited fishing on Sunday, a waste because the fish remained in the river just a short time.

In private houses, grace was said before the meat was eaten. Usually all the courses, even dessert, were put on the table at once. Tablecloths fell over the knees and took the place of napkins, in the English style.

Baltimore, America's fourth largest city with 13,000 people, was dark with badly paved streets. In Boston, the third largest city in America with a population of 18,000, everything reminded travelers of London—the brick and wooden houses, the customs, even the accent. The second largest city with a population of 33,000, New York still showed the ravages of war. It had been occupied by the enemy for seven years. Now the wharves were in poor repair. A great fire had swept away almost every building on Broadway. Philadelphia's population of 43,000 made it the nation's largest metropolis. Its growth had been phenomenal. Moreover, the city was looked upon as urbane and cultured.

European visitors continually expressed surprise at the equality between citizens of different rank. "People treat us very familiarly," wrote a Frenchman, "and they do it so innocently that we should be very hard to get on with if we took it in bad part." In Boston, the governor of the state himself answered their knock when Europeans came to call.

As for the stagecoach drivers, they were unique. They might be addressed as major, their rank during the Revolutionary War, and be asked to pass on all sorts of matters as though they were judges. And Europeans remarked on the pleasure of traveling everywhere unchallenged by customs officials or seigneurs demanding a toll for passing over their land.

The almost classless society impressed Europeans. Thomas Cooper said that there were no Americans of great rank, not many of great riches. "Nor have the rich the power of oppressing the less rich, for poverty such as in Great Britain is almost unknown." The word *farmer*, explained Cooper, had in America a new meaning. While in England it meant a tenant paying rent and doomed to an inferior rank in life, in Pennsylvania, a farmer was a landowner, equal to any man in the state.

Both French and English visitors marveled at the lack of distinction in dress between maid and mistress and the lower orders and the leaders of the state. "Luxury," wrote one, "has penetrated to the cottage of the workingman."

Along the Atlantic coastline, newspapers were numerous, although not in "the great interior country," as Gouverneur Morris called it. There, few schools existed as well.

However, Transylvania College had been founded "beyond the mountains." Even before 1780 at least 17 colleges had existed in America. After the war, they sprang up everywhere. The best known of the older institutions remained Harvard, William and Mary, Yale, Columbia, and Princeton. The Library Company in Philadelphia probably had the best library in America. The city also boasted the American Philosophical Society, a learned group established by Benjamin Franklin "for the promotion of useful knowledge."

By the 1780s every state but Delaware had chartered at least one university. Many academies were founded (especially in New England) to furnish instruction at the secondary level, and sometimes beyond, to both boys and girls.

Doctors prescribed red bark, laudanum, and opium; they applied blisters and clysters, measured out vomits and cathartics, and bled their patients for fevers and almost anything else. No wonder that people did not call for the doctor unless they were desperate. Home remedies included rhubarb and senna, castor oil, Daffy's Elixir, tea made of quashey root or nettles, and plasters made of honey and flour, onion, garlic, and deer fat.

Visitors also commented eloquently on American women. Some found the Boston girls prettiest, but others voted for the Philadelphia belles. The Frenchman Moreau de Saint-Mery wrote that on a fine day, along the north sidewalk of Market Street between Third and Fifth in Philadelphia, "one can see four hundred young persons, each of whom would certainly be followed on any Paris promenade." Unfortunately, he added, they will be "faded at twenty-three, old at thirty-five, decrepit at forty-five."

Foreigners marveled at the prudery of most American ma-
trons. Moreau de Saint-Mery said he had seen a woman make her
brother leave the room while she changed the diaper of her five-
week-old son. American women never used in public the words
garter, leg, knee, or shirt. They divided their body in two—the
stomach was from the head to the waist, the rest was ankles. A
doctor must have despaired at learning the place of the malady in
a female patient.

Women left the table at the end of dessert and normally did
not expect to join in male conversation, to the astonishment of the
French traveler, but not to the British. However, even the British
remarked at the shyness of most American women. Respectable
ladies did not perform in public, even in the church choir, although
this taboo was beginning to break down, as Webster discovered.

Foreigners were finding what was and still is normal in a new
civilization and world: rigidity, clannishness, and suspicion of the
stranger. They found equality, but not easy gaiety and laughter, and
not an absence of prudery.

"I do not think America is the place for a man of pleasure,"
wrote Thomas Cooper. Even in Philadelphia he said he knew of
only one "professed gentleman—i.e., idle, unoccupied person of
fortune. Their time is not yet come."

Even such wealthy men as Thomas Jefferson rarely remained
idle. This was the era of the multitalented individual, like Jefferson
or Benjamin Franklin. The conditions of life demanded it and the
era's rationalism encouraged it. Jefferson became an architect because he could find none in America. He built a fine library because
Virginia had none. He learned to play the violin because musicians
rarely visited him.

When Webster took to the road, his trip helped broaden him
so that he could, also, become a multifaceted man.

Chapter 9

THE TRAVELING MAN

On May 2, 1785, Noah Webster arrived in New Haven on the first leg of his 13-month tour.

In his diary he noted that he saw a balloon ascend, which may have served as a good omen for his trip, although the sober school-teacher, lawyer, and author would never have admitted it. Nevertheless, it impressed him enough to devote 13 words to the event —comparatively verbose for this laconic document.

This was the period of the first balloon ascensions. Ballooning was the rage in Paris, and the phenomenon was introduced to America by Benjamin Franklin. When someone asked Franklin, "What is the use of this new invention?" he replied, "What is the use of a newborn baby?"

Webster was, in the terminology of twentieth-century advertising, sending up a trial balloon, too, because he didn't yet know what he would do with his life, let alone what this trip would accomplish.

The South was the land of opportunity for the young intellectuals of the North, especially those from New England. Many teachers and writers who found the going difficult in the North, met a warmer welcome in the South, which still suffered from a shortage of teachers and educated young men. Abraham Baldwin, tutor to Yale's class of 1780 and Joel Barlow's brother-in-law, rose to prominence in Georgia, where voters sent him to the Constitutional Convention in 1787. And Noah's classmate, Josiah Meigs, was to become the president of the University of Georgia.

After Webster's second attempt at founding a school in Sharon failed in 1782, he had hoped to go South. Three years later, he made good his plans, aiming to introduce his books in other states, secure copyrights, and promote American nationalism.

Josiah Blakeley, a Hartford friend, had persuaded Noah that Baltimore would best serve as his headquarters during his forays into the South. Although Webster found the city unattractive compared to Hartford, he used it as his homing point. He particularly thought its Sunday behavior indecent, when "hundreds of blacks collected for pastime, cracking their whips, elevating kites into the air, breaking each others' heads with clubs, and alarming whole streets with their quarrels."

Noah Webster had a puppylike curiosity about all the new sights and experiences. Typical is his journal for the first few days of July 1785:

Got under way early & arrive in Charleston at 8 oclock—Lodge at Mr. Welsh's at sign of the cross keyes in King Street. Happy to find shore & good provision. Go to St. Michael's Church; hear Parson Smith & Miss Storrer sing. She sung a part of the Oratorio of the Messiah; the organ joined. An odd affair this, for a woman to sing for benefit; but I put a quarter of a dollar into the plate. She sung well in the modern taste, but I cannot admire it. I went to the White meeting P.M. & heard the New England method of psalm sing. Heard part of a Methodist sermon in the evening. The people of Charleston are very civil & polite. They behave with great decency at church, & the slaves attend in greater numbers & behave with more decorum that I have seen in America.

Back in Baltimore by mid-July, Noah shows a little relief at being back in more familiar surroundings and following more customary pursuits:

Lodge at Mrs. Sanderson's, with my N England friends. Wait on Dr. Allison—who offers me his church for the use of a singing school.

Sunday. At home, which is very uncommon. PM introduced to Mrs. Blanchard, Miss Blanchard, Mr. Johonnot, Dr. Mills &c; take tea at Mr. Blanchard's & a walk.

Arrange some private matters. Procure Telemachus in. French & English & a master to teach me.

By November, he was beginning to hit his stride, on a trip to Virginia:

Dine at Mr. Herberts.

Dine with Mr. McWhir, an Irish literary Gentleman, who keeps the Academy; pass the evening with him & Dr. Swift.

Ride from Alexandria to Fredericksburg, about 70 miles.

To Richmond, 70 miles.

Lodge at Mrs. Allegre's. Wait on Dr. Stewart, on Mr. Moses Austin; take tea with him. Introduced to Mr. Mumford, to Mr. Clarkson from New Jersey.

Webster's diaries of this time also display his interest in statistics. He counted the number of houses in a town (230 in Williamsburg, 300 in Petersburg), and made precise notations about the weather and temperatures. He could be called America's first amateur census taker; indeed, his journals have been used as the source for estimates of local populations in the 1780s. He continued as well a farmer's son's interest in meteorology until his death.

Noah Webster's touring method was to collect letters of introduction to prominent people in the city or area he proposed to visit. Once there, he would persuade the worthies whom he had thus met to pass him on to other prominent people in the region. His diaries read like a Who's Who for 1785–86. Scarcely a day passed when he did not take tea, dine, or breakfast with someone of note. Sometimes he had a meal with three different people on the same day. He arrived in Annapolis, Maryland, on January 1, 1786. His diary records his peripatetic days:

January 1. Sunday. Lodge at Mr. Mann's. Wait on Dr. Shuttleworth with letter.

2 Breakfast with him, introduced to Mr. Quinn.

3 Introduced to Governor Smallwood, a very good kind of Character. . . . Introduced to Major Lynch, an Irishman.

4 Write, go to Assembly, dance with Mrs. Davison, wife of an honest Scotchman. A brilliant circle of ladies.

General Washington received him cordially and invited him to spend the night at Mount Vernon. Noah gave him a copy of his *Sketches* and discussed subjects of interest—the need for a strong central government, abolition of slavery, farming, and education. Webster amused the general when at dinner he refused a serving of molasses with the remark, "We have enough of that in our country." He referred to the "slow as molasses" procedures in Congress.

But Webster was no sycophant. While he was visiting Washington a short while later (to secure introductory letters to people at Richmond), the general mentioned that he sought someone from Scotland to serve as his secretary and as a tutor to Mrs. Washington's Custis grandchildren.

Noah's nationalism bristled, and he chided his host for not seeking an American for the post. The general agreed and asked for nominees. Webster promised to investigate. Later, it occurred to him that he could handle the assignment and nominated himself, but his letter shows the indecisiveness that troubled him at this period:

"If I understood you, Sir, it is your wish to find a suitable person and employ him for a number of years. I am so far advanced in life and have so far accomplished my wishes that I have no idea of continuing single for any long period. My circumstances do not require it, and my feelings forbid it."

Even Noah recognized that he sounded pompous, so he added, "You will perhaps smile, Sir, at the expression; but if I am frank, I am certainly not singular."

The general hired someone else, Tobias Lear, an American.

Humor was not Webster's long suit. When he showed it, it was often unconscious, as in the foregoing letter, or in the form of heavy-handed sarcasm, as occasionally found in his polemical writing.

In the lectures that Webster had developed during his tour, he showed a sarcastic brilliance in squelching hecklers. He could silence most of them by calling them "macerated pre-admonites" or "convoluted stomatopods." But he got some of this back in kind. One critic described him as "a pusillanimous, half-begotten, self-dubbed patriot." At least he was becoming known.

Two ventures that Webster had attempted in Baltimore to earn money and reputation had come to little; he had tried to open an elementary school without success and had managed to start a singing school, but in several instances had had to take such payment as gloves and wine because of the shortage of currency. Characteristically, Noah turned even the shortage to account by writing an article in which he laid the problem more fundamentally to a deficiency in the union of the states.

The singing school episode also had one disagreeable incident.

In his diary Webster noted "a miff between Mr. Hall—a singer—and myself. People in Baltimore have not been accustomed to my rigid discipline."

Early in his stay at Baltimore Webster attended the lectures of Dr. Henry Moyes, the blind Scottish scientist, who spoke on various natural phenomena. It occurred to Noah that he could lecture on the science of language. Accordingly, he began writing lectures, basing his remarks on some of his material in the *Institute* and on his wide reading. He modified and improved these over the months. By July 12, 1786, there appeared this outline of his lectures as an ad in *The Massachusetts Centinel:*

I. Introduction. Origin of the English Language. Derivation of the European Languages from the ancient Celtic. History of English.

II. Elements of the English Language. Rules of Pronunciation. Different dialects of the Eastern, the Middle, and the Southern States.

III. Some Differences between the English and Americans considered. Corruption of Language in England. Reasons why the English should not be our Standard, either in Language or Manners.

IV. Prevailing Errors in use of Words. Errors of Grammarians in arrangement of the Verbs. Consequences of these in the most correct Writings.

V. Poetry. Principles of English Verse explained. Use and effect of the several Pauses. Effects of different poetic Measures illustrated by examples.

VI. General Remarks on Education. Defects in our mode of Education. Influence of Education on Morals and of Morals on Government. Female Education. Connection between the Mode of Education and the form of Government. Effects of an European Education in America. Tour of America a useful Branch of Education.

Webster charged 12 shillings for the entire series of six lectures, or 3 shillings for just one lecture. Women had to pay just 6 shillings for the entire course but 3 shillings for one lecture. These discourses eventually became the basis of *Dissertations on the English Language* (published in 1789) and *A Collection of Essays and Fugitiv Writings* (published in 1790), two neglected but important American books.

Noah gave his first lecture on October 19, 1785, and attracted only 30 listeners. However, the numbers increased thereafter, and this activity became his main means of support while on tour.

Lecturing in those days was not the decorous experience we now usually associate with the activity. On June 6, 1786, he gave his talks in his hometown Hartford, reading them to the state's general assembly. He had given tickets to the legislators. Some citizens, irate either at not having received free tickets or at the memories of what he had written earlier, broke windows. An indignant Webster noted in his diary: "Let it be remembered that in the year 1786, there are people in Hartford so illiberal, that they will not permit public Lectures to be read in a church because they cannot be admitted without paying!"

His lectures on language proved neither a rousing success nor an abject failure. In a letter he reports on the up-and-down nature of his audiences: "I read my Lectures to few friends in Hartford, but most people paid no attention to them. . . . In New Haven I have about 70 hearers, consisting of the best families in town, and a few scholars; a greater number in proportion to the size of the town than I have had before; and they seem more pleased with the plan than any audience I have had."

Webster thought well of his abilities as a lecturer. But a more objective listener, Timothy Pickering, had reservations. Pickering had served as quartermaster general of the Revolutionary Army in 1783 and was to be postmaster general in 1791, secretary of state from 1795 to 1800 and still later a U. S. Senator and member of the House of Representatives from Massachusetts. He wrote to a friend that Noah "possessed a quantum sufficit of vanity, so that he really overrated his own talents. He imagined that he was a good reader, but I had so much friendship for him as to point out his defects; and though it was evidently a little mortifying, he thanked me then, and has since made his acknowledgements by letter. He was particularly defective in reading poetry, and this perhaps as much as anything disgusted his audience."

Indeed, it would take a man of Pickering's stature to get Webster's respectful attention. Noah never did take criticism well. If he had not been trying to cultivate Pickering at the time and if he didn't genuinely respect the man 13 years older than he, he probably would have written him off as one of his enemies—a list that was already beginning to grow.

The lectures expanded the principles he had presented in the three parts of the *Institute.* He repeated his conclusions that English was a Teutonic and not a Latin language as erroneously supposed. Webster asked that Americans examine their own usage as the basis for textbook principles in the study of their language. He had listened to the popular speech of every state, and he had concluded that "the people of America, in particular the English descendants, speak the most *pure English* now known in the world." This was no xenophobic conclusion. A people migrating from a homeland, insulated by a large ocean from contact with the evolving mother tongue, will preserve the speech they carried with them when they left. Noah wrote:

> Let Englishmen notice that when I speak of the American yeomanry, the latter are not to be compared to the illiterate peasantry of their own country. The yeomanry of this country consists of substantial independent freeholders, masters of their own persons and lords of their own soil. These men have considerable education. They not only learn to read, write, and keep accounts; but a vast proportion of them read newspapers every week, and besides the Bible, which is found in all families, they read the best English sermons and treatises upon religion, ethics, geography and history; such as the works of Watts, Addison, Atterbury, Salmon, etc. In the eastern states there are public schools sufficient to instruct every man's children, and most of the children are actually benefited by these institutions. The people of distant counties in England can hardly understand one another, so various are their dialects; but in the extent of twelve hundred miles in America, there are very few, I question whether a hundred words, such as are used in employments wholly local, which are not universally intelligible.

Webster pointed out that the great number of immigrants pouring into America created a number of dialects that might weaken the perfection of American speech. He argued that the establishment of schools "and some uniformity in the use of books can annihilate differences of speaking and preserve the purity of the American tongue." He concluded: "Let us then seize the present moment, and establish a *national* language, as well as a national government."

The unifying agents that America lacked in the 1780s were a national language, the institution of schools, and a national government. Webster set about to establish all three. But he recognized the difficulties, especially with education. Webster wrote in his diary for January 6, 1786:

Converse with Mr. Lloyd, a senator—a sensible man from the Eastern Shore. He informs me that great numbers of men who acknowledge deeds before him cannot write their names. This is the case in Maryland & Virginia. An eminent merchant in Alexandria informed me that of fifty planters in Virginia, who sold him Tobacco, four or five only could write their names but made a mark on the receipts. O New England! how superior are thy inhabitants in morals, literature, civility & industry.

In a letter to Pickering on January 20, 1786, from Baltimore, Noah wrote:

I have now finished my business in these states, having secured the copy right of my works and introduced them into the schools. I have also read Lectures in the Principal Towns in Virginia and Maryland . . . My success has encouraged me to proceed, and I shall risque my reputation in Philadelphia, New York, and Boston, upon the merits and strength of my criticisms. I shall make one *General* effort to deliver literature and my countrymen from the errors that fashion and ignorance are palming upon Englishmen. . . . I must wait on the Legislature of Delaware, and shall, I expect, be in Philadelphia by the tenth of February. Two circumstances will operate against me. I am not a *foreigner;* I am a *New Englandman.* A foreigner ushered in with titles and letters, with half my abilities would have the whole city in his train. But let my fate be what it will, I am convinced I am right, and have had the good fortune to convince every good judge who has heard me, that I proceed on true principles.

In Philadelphia and New York Noah encountered more sophisticated audiences. A friendly critic commented on his stiff delivery: "His voice is clear and distinct, but not very flexible or harmonious. . . . The style is both concise and forcible . . . and although divested of flowers of rhetorick, yet it may be considered as tolerably elegant." The critic noted Webster's New England pronunciation—*lecter* for lecture and *Edurd* for Edward—and found fault, as Pickering had, with his reading of poetry: "Mr. Webster speaks too quick, too much in the same tone, and raises his voice and pauses too long at the end of every line. He appears to be enraptured when he speaks, but his raptures seem forced."

Noah replied by correcting stylistic errors in the critic's comment. The mild attack may have prompted him to get a puff printed in *The Daily Advertiser* in New York: "It is strange that curiosity should be so dormant and partial to an American in his own country. The Lectures of Mr. Webster, although of much public and private utility, do not seem to meet the encouragement in this city they so evidently deserve."

Moving on to Schenectady and Albany, Webster had smaller audiences because "the Dutch have no taste for the English language." His Hartford reception depressed him. When he reached the northernmost point of this travels, Portsmouth, New Hampshire, he had a reunion with his old Yale tutor, Joseph Buckminster, but was saddened to find him ill.

Even though audiences picked up as he traveled through New England, he grew dispirited by another event. His trip happened to coincide with Shays' Rebellion. Disaffected farmers and other citizens prevented the Courts of Common Pleas from sitting in western Massachusetts. Although the uprising didn't develop into civil war, it showed Webster again the urgent need for a more effective central government.

He dashed off more anonymous articles on the subject. In the Newburyport, Massachusetts, paper, *The Essex Journal,* on September 13, 1786, appeared this observation: "Were I at the head of the Executiv authority, I should soon put the question to a decisiv issue. It should be determined, on the first insurrection, whether our lives and our properties should be secured under the law and constitution of the State, or whether they must seek for tranquility in some distant country." (Note the dropping of the final *e* in some words, symptomatic of his Franklin-influenced forays into simplified spelling.)

In another article, in *The United States Chronicle* of Providence, he published a bitterly sarcastic piece under the pseudonym "Tom Thoughtful": "But when mobs and conventions oppose the courts of justice, and Legislatures make paper or old horses a legal tender in all cases, the world will exclaim with one voice—*Ye are rogues, and the devil is in you!"*

This article was widely reprinted throughout New England and helped stem the tide of insurrection. But Webster had become disillusioned about New England. In May 1785 he had left Hartford, convinced of the superiority of all things New England. His 13 months abroad and Shays' Rebellion had brought a sea change in him. On November 20, 1786, he went so far as to write in *The Connecticut Courant:* "I was once as strong a republican as any man in America. Now, a republican is among the last kinds of government I should choose. I would infinitely prefer a limited monarchy, for I would sooner be the subject of the caprice of one man than to the ignorance and passions of the multitude."

This view foreshadows a later position. He remained an ardent American nationalist, however, and the Philadelphia Constitutional Convention revived his hopes in a great America. He was headed for Philadelphia where another chapter in the nation's history was about to unfold.

Chapter 10

THE PHILADELPHIA INTERSECTION

Like many other intelligent Americans, Noah Webster had grown thoroughly alarmed at the new nation's political and economic conditions by the end of 1786. Furthermore, his own personal fortunes remained at a low ebb. Besides wavering in his personal political ideals, he had no regular job. His tour had increased his personal debt, and he still could not repay his father fully for his college education.

Webster loved to teach, but he felt that teaching in a secondary school was beneath a nationally known lecturer and author. Indeed, he had succeeded on his tour in introducing the *Institute* throughout the 13 states, but he had so far reaped little financial benefit. Although he knew the long-term folly of the practice, he needed ready cash so urgently that he sold short-term rights to his books for ridiculously low sums.

Noah vacillated about what he should do. He half refused General Washington's tutorial-secretarial job at the same time that he applied for it. He could have had the chair of oratory at the University of Pennsylvania, but he objected to the long hours of monitorial work, so the post went to another. He had a date to visit Benjamin Franklin in Philadelphia to discuss a phonetic alphabet, and he wrote Franklin an ambivalent letter, typical of his indecision at this time, that half applied for a job and half informed him that he was too busy with his many projects to accept a full-time position: "I wish for business—it is my life—it is my pleasure, as well as my support. . . . But I began a vast design without a shilling, and I know the world too well to ask pecuniary assistance from any person. I want none, I will take none but what I earn. I wish, if possible, to have business which will afford me some leisure, for my lectures must be prepared for the press as soon as possible, and my *Institute* stands in need of improvement."

Franklin didn't know what to make of all this, so wisely said nothing.

Webster had dined with and been accepted by the great and wealthy of America during his tour. He felt entitled to a position of honor that paid commensurately. He felt somehow cheated that he hadn't gotten it in Hartford, so he left his birthplace on Thanksgiving Day in 1786 "perhaps for life," he wrote in his diary.

Nor did he find a job in New Haven, although the worthies of Yale did help him to get his political thinking straight again. He departed for New York, once more convinced that the republican form of government would best serve America. In New York, he looked for a job for two weeks without success.

Perhaps Webster was sublimating his personal disappointments by writing essays such as this:

The philosopher will felicitate himself with the prospect of discoveries favorable to arts and happiness; the statesman will rejoice that there is a retreat from the vassalage of Europe; the divine will bless God that a place had been reserved for an uncorrupted church; and the philanthropist, who compares the yeomanry of America with the peasantry of Europe, will congratulate himself on an event which has removed millions of people from the ambition of princes, and from the participation of the vices, which mark the decline of nations.

He concluded with a theme that would dominate his writings for the rest of his days: The Revolution had not been completed by a military victory; it was continuing by other means.

On Christmas Day in 1786 Webster set off for Philadelphia, three months late for his appointment with Franklin.

Noah's first business was not politics but phonetics. He and Franklin had had long discussions and correspondence about the subject. Webster never went as far as Franklin in advocating cabalistic symbols for some of the sounds in English because he knew too much already about language and about the innate conservatism of most people concerning the tongue they had learned at their mother's knee. But he did advocate simplified spelling.

He proposed three simple rules: First, omit all superfluous or silent letters. So, *bread, head, give, breast, built, meant, realm,* and *friend* would be spelled *bred, hed, giv, brest, bilt, ment, relm,* and *frend.*

Second, substitute a character that has a definite sound for one that is vague or indeterminate. Thus, he substituted *ee* for *ea* or *ie* in order to form *meen, neer, greev, speek,* and *zeel.* By this process, he also achieved *greef, kee, beleev, laf, dawter, plow, tuf, proov, blud,* and *draft.* For *ch* in Greek derivatives he substituted *k,* with *karacter, korus, kolic,* and *arkitecture* resulting. The *ch* in French derivatives would become *sh.* Therefore, *machine, chaise,* and *chevalier* would be spelled *masheen, shaze,* and *shevaleer.* The *ch* in such English derivatives as *cherish* would not change.

Third, distinguish between different sounds spelled the same way with "a trifling alternation in a character or the addition of a point" to note the difference. For example, the two sounds of *th* in *the* and *theater* would be differentiated by putting a small stroke across one of them. A point or other mark over vowels, such as *à* or *i,* would differentiate them.

Webster devoted several years to defending this system, which won Franklin's blessing. The diplomat stood always ready to back down from extreme positions to accomplish a practical result.

However, Webster himself gradually abandoned most of his reforms. He never introduced many of them into his spellers, wisely recognizing the danger of upsetting the established spelling order. However, many went into his 1806 dictionary, although they began to disappear in the 1807 and 1810 dictionaries for schools. They were removed wholesale in the great 1828 dictionary, and even more were removed from the 1841 edition.

A few of Webster's reforms survive to this day, at least in American usage: *-or* and *-er* endings, not *-our* and *-re* as in *honor* and *center;* dropping the superfluous ending *e* or *k* as in *ax* instead of *axe* or *music* instead of *musick;* or dropping the double consonant as in *traveler* instead of *traveller;* or spelling closer to the actual sound as in *plow* instead of *plough.*

While Webster's suggestions did not result in wholesale reform, they accomplished some lasting simplifications. This is more than can be said for most of the ideas of other spelling reformers before or after him.

Webster's association with Franklin also had political results. Noah became a Franklin protegé, and Franklin knew everyone worth knowing in America. Webster may have traded on the friendship too widely, irritating some of those native and temporary Philadelphians who flocked to the city to be on hand either as delegates or as hangers-on for the Constitutional Convention beginning in May. Indeed, he may have given just cause for dislike among some. On February 17, 1787, he noted in his diary that he engaged in a scuffle while taking tea. But he felt remorse because he also recorded: "In a boyish scuffle with Mr. Blanchard, tho against my will; a chair is broke; folly in little boys is excusable, but in great boys it is odious."

William Cobbett, a writer who was to plague Noah for many years, probably invented one piece of Websterian apocrypha. Dr. Benjamin Rush, whom Noah had cultivated, supposedly met him upon his arrival and said: "How do you do, my dear friend. I congratulate you on your arrival in Philadelphia." "Sir," Webster allegedly replied, "you may congratulate Philadelphia on the occasion." (Even in his grave, Cobbett pursued Noah. In his will, Cobbett bequeathed five pounds to Noah to pay for a new engraving of his portrait, so that the children who used his speller might no longer be frightened out of their wits by the grim Websterian visage.)

With Franklin's support, Webster tried to resurrect his lecture series, but this failed. Finally in April 1787 he accepted a position as master of the English language in the recently organized Episcopal Academy at 200 pounds to be paid in paper currency. This development aroused the derision of Thomas Freeman, writing in *The Freeman's Journal:*

The uncertainty of all human affairs never appeared more manifestly than in the case of Noah Webster, jun. esq., whose extraordinary abilities and unparalleled knowledge of the English language, have enabled him to write that masterpiece of instruction, his *Grammatical Institute.* His consciousness of his own great learning and genius, had justly led him to imagine, that, by his becoming an itinerant lecturer through the United States, he would, by this means, be one of the most valuable citizens of our new empire, and have his name ranked among the great men of this western world.—But, alas! all his well-digested plans and schemes have vanished into smoke, his *learned* and *useful lectures* have been neglected, and he himself suffered to starve, or to join one of the most Herculean pieces of labor that ever poor man engaged in, to wit, that of a schoolmaster.

Other scurrilous newspaper attacks appeared in answer to Webster's prolific pen. His quickness to reply to all slurs was one reason for the attention given him. Another reason was that there was little else to write about. No news came from the Constitutional Convention, whose members were pledged to secrecy. About the only source of leaks was the garrulous Franklin, at whose table Webster frequently dined.

Furthermore, General Washington, elected chairman of the Convention, paid a personal call on Webster on May 26, only two days after the delegates had formally convened. Washington had been successful in persuading the members to probe to the very bottom of the Articles of Confederation, not to confine themselves to superficial changes. Webster had argued for this fundamental revision in his *Sketches of American Policy* and in his lectures.

In his diary during the Convention that ran from May 24 to September 17, Webster reports visiting or dining with many other members: James Madison, Rufus King, Abraham Baldwin, Edmund Randolph, William Samuel Johnson, Oliver Ellsworth, Roger Sherman, and William Livingston. In the entry for August 23, he notes: "Pass evening at Mr. Marshall's, with Convention Gentlemen,"

Most likely during these social occasions his ideas were mentioned. Webster himself had become something of an after-diner conversationalist.

On September 15, two days before the Convention finished its work, Thomas Fitzsimmons, a delegate from Pennsylvania, wrote Webster a letter requesting that he prepare an essay to support the new Constitution, "from a conviction that your abilities may be eminently useful on the present occasion." Fitzsimmons went on: "If unreasonable jealousies are disseminated, its [the new Constitution's] adoption may at least be protracted. In my mind to delay is to destroy."

In response to Fitzsimmons' request, Webster wrote a pamphlet defending the new Constitution and urging its adoption. It bore this title in the lengthy style so dear to eighteenth-century authors: *An Examination into the Leading Principles of the Federal Constitution proposed by the late Convention held at Philadelphia. With Answers to the Principal Objections that have been raised against the System. By a Citizen of America.* He wrote it on October 8 and 9, dedicating it to Franklin. A week later it was printed and distributed throughout Philadelphia and the nation. Although Webster's name didn't appear, the author's identity was widely known. Dr. David Ramsay wrote from Charleston: "I have read it with pleasure, and it is now in brisk circulation among my friends. I have heard every person who has read it express his high approbation of its contents. It will doubtless be of singular service in recommending the adoption of the New Constitution."

Years later, Webster wrote on the pamphlet's flyleaf, "This is a hasty production." While true, it offers examples of Websterian polemical prose at its best:

They [mutual sacrifices of states' sovereignties] *must* be made sooner or later by every state, or jealousies, local interests, and prejudices will unsheath the sword and some Caesar or Cromwell will avail himself of our divisions and wade to a throne through steams of blood. . . . But the Americans must cease to contend, to fear, and to hate before they can realize the benefits of independence and government or enjoy the blessings which heaven has lavished in rich profusion upon this western world.

The haste also made it among the first public writings to support the Constitution. From start to finish, Noah Webster played a significant role in the formulation of the Constitution. If he had little influence in actually writing the document, he first—and almost alone—had phrased the basic concept on which it should be founded. He alone had sounded the call to continental union from Charleston, South Carolina, to Portsmouth, New Hampshire. His presence in Philadelphia during the Convention and his frequent meetings with Franklin and other delegates must have had some effect on the Constitution itself. But above all, he helped create a public opinion favorable to the success of the Convention.

Why then has Webster's role been largely forgotten? A clue to the answer may lie in a comment by Sir Francis Bacon in the sixteenth century: "Always let losers have their words." Webster

never learned that wisdom. As a polemicist, he tried to so over-
whelm his opponents that they would forever be silenced. He
seldom silenced them, of course. As a result, he carried on feuds
for so long that everyone but the immediate parties grew sick of
them.

Even his friends found him trying. When a critic called him a
"sciolist" (a person whose learning is superficial), he replied with
a 64-page pamphlet. He was a "stiff" young man, a self-sufficient
introvert with great energy and gifts for using that energy effectively. He constantly, although unwittingly, alienated supporters.
Although contentious, he was not quarrelsome, self-confident but
not vain. Yet, his contemporaries often tended to see him less
favorably. If he never showed petty animosities toward others, he
had a genius for arousing them against himself.

Fortunately, Webster was tough and self-assured enough to
battle singlehandedly against all opposition. In fact, dispraise
spurred him to great labor and accomplishment. A diary notation
of this period says: "I have exposed myself to malice, envy, criticism
etc. by my publications. I knew I should when I began and I am
prepared for an attack on all sides."

Although Webster always considered himself nonpartisan politically, others saw him increasingly as one of the more contentious
Federalists. Indeed, he had swung to the views of the Federalist
majority in the Convention. He had come to believe that popular
sovereignty should be limited to electing members of the House of
Representatives and that the electors themselves should have no
right to control the votes of their representatives. He believed that
the Senate should sit in judgment upon resolutions of the House,
thus preventing the "sudden and violent passions" of the common
people from stilling "the voice of freedom."

With other Federalists, Webster thought a Bill of Rights un-
needed, substituting for it rights based on property. This may seem
strange in a man with heavy debts, but he defined "property"
broadly. For him it meant "without indigence." In those days,
indigence meant more than poverty; it also meant a life without
prospects of any material improvement. One without such prospects in the yeasty atmosphere of the new Republic was indeed
beyond the pale. Since Noah always had the prospect, if not the
actuality, of material prosperity, he felt himself to be without indi-

gence, hence a man of property qualified to participate in and comment on the new government.

Webster made still another important connection in Philadelphia. He met there his future wife, Rebecca Greenleaf, who was visiting from Boston. Although he had a lifelong bias against "society," that is, the wellborn, he overlooked the fact that his Becca had been born well. Actually, he objected more to the manners of some society members. In a Philadelphia diary notation, he wrote: "Go to the Assembly; the Ladies will not dance with strangers, if they can avoid it—polite indeed! People in high life suppose they can dispense with the rules of civility."

But Rebecca showed eminent civility, as most ladies did to him. He liked women and enjoyed their company—perhaps more than he enjoyed the society of men. There is no record that he ever quarreled with a woman, although his battles with men were numerous. In the early years of his diary, references like this are common: ". . . In the evening was a multitude of pretty faces."

"At home. Read a little, loitered some, had some company, and visited the Ladies in the evening as usual."

"Mortified to find my eyes too weak to study. But if I cannot devote my time to books, I can to the Ladies."

He met Rebecca Greenleaf in March 1787 when she was visiting her sister, Mrs. Duncan Ingraham, in Philadelphia. On March 1 he was introduced to her; on the seventh she was "the sweet Miss Greenleaf," on the ninth, "the agreeable Miss Greenleaf." By the 22nd, she was the "lovely Becca." By June, when she returned home to Boston, they knew they wanted to marry.

Rebecca Greenleaf was the 13th of 15 children of William and Mary Greenleaf. William, descended from French Huguenots, had been a prosperous merchant before the Revolutionary War, but the British blockade ruined his business, and he never recovered economically. Nevertheless, he remained a staunch patriot. The family suffered great hardship under the British occupation of Boston during the war.

William Greenleaf was a genial, affectionate father, much loved by his family. Mary Greenleaf, Becca's mother, was a stern, society-conscious woman whom her children recalled with reserve.

Becca was pretty and sprightly. She had bright, dark eyes and hair and straight small features. A granddaughter recalls, "She was

little of stature, and of light weight, but was very erect and graceful.''

Rebecca's brother James was also visiting the Ingrahams. Noah
and the brother became good friends; James later served as a sponsor for Webster as he tried to persuade the family that the author
could support their daughter.

In a letter to James, who was then in Europe pursuing his
export-import business, Webster wrote: "I wish for a home, I wish
for a companion. To these considerations I may add that marriage
makes a man a more respectable citizen; it gives him credit and
business." Perhaps realizing that such sentiments scarcely showed
him as an ardent lover, Noah continued more conventionally:

If there ever was a woman, moulded by the hand of nature to bless her
friends in all connections, it is your sister B. . . . To be united to her is
not mere pleasure, bliss, felicity, it is more, it is a union that blends
pleasure and delight with social advantages, it is a blessing. The man who
loves her, loves the temper of saints, and by associating with her, must
become a better man, a better citizen, a warmer friend. His heart must be
softened by her virtues, his benevolent & tender affections must be multi-
plied. In short, he must be good, for he would be, in some measure, like
her.

Noah Webster now, more than ever, had incentive to make a
material success of something. He had given up the Academy teaching job as unsatisfactory. He had an idea for still another venture
that he saw would draw on all his varied experience.

Chapter 11

ON THE ROAD

On October 16, 1787, Noah Webster wrote in his diary: "My birthday. 29 years of my life gone! I have been industrious—endeavored to do some good, & hope I shall be able to correct my faults & yet do more good. Put my trunk aboard for N York."

Noah was starting still another experiment in his quest for a life goal. He had written books and articles, taught school, practiced law and lectured. Now he proposed to edit a magazine.

Regional magazines were already established in Philadelphia, New Haven, and Boston. Webster chose to begin one in New York. With his customary prescience he foresaw the growth of that city. He defended his choice to his friend Dr. Benjamin Rush, who had urged him to consider Philadelphia:

> The place I have chosen for publishing it is not the seat of literature; but Philadelphia furnishes two periodical publications & to begin another there would be neither generous nor eligible. New York will always be the destination of the Packets, & the facility of the intercourse with all parts of America gives it a preference, which can never be rivalled. I can send to several ports of the Union two or three weeks sooner from New York, than from Philadelphia, a great advantage. The Philadelphia publications will never have much circulation in the eastern States, that is, in one third of the Union. Mine circulates through the whole.

With his usual optimism at the start of all new ventures, Webster signed an agreement with Samuel Loudon, a New York printer, to print the new publication to be called *The American*

Magazine. Dr. Rush urged that he change the name because "American" connoted failure, suggesting instead "Monthly Asylum" (an interesting example of words changing meaning), but Webster wisely refused to do so. Although Noah had not yet started, or perhaps even contemplated, a dictionary, he was already enough of a lexicographer to reject that proposal.

Webster had by then grown in experience and maturity. When he wrote his speller, grammar, and reader, he accepted the bad advice of Dr. Stiles of Yale to entitle the series *The Institute.* Then he was swayed by Stiles' prestige. Even though Rush was older than Webster and had more national standing than Stiles possessed, Noah this time held his ground.

The printer Samuel Loudon, experienced and wise, demanded cash in advance, so Webster again had to sell rights to his *Institute* for five years to raise the money. The shady Samuel Campbell won the lucrative contract. Webster remained optimistic about the magazine. His travels in Connecticut, and his letters and advertisements in New York, Philadelphia, Charleston, and Boston gave him a promised circulation of 500, sufficient to pay printing costs and to ensure a good profit.

In organizing the magazine, Webster arranged his material under topics, such as government, antiquities, essays, reviews, agriculture, theology, poetry, and news. Selections were usually short, so the publication had a modern digest quality.

The American Magazine immediately demonstrated its superiority over its rivals. It first presented a comprehensive theory of education, an able presentation of governmental problems, and truly distinguished literary criticism. It was the first real magazine of discussion in America.

Everet A. Duyckinck's *Cyclopedia of American Literature* of 1875 said it was "a creditable though unsuccessful pioneer attempt in this department of literature. It was neat in its arrangement and though 'miscellaneous' in its contents, started some interesting antiquarian and scientific matters in the Editor's letter to President Stiles on Western fortifications and other topics. Its Americanism was well sustained by poetical extracts from Dwight, Barlow and Trumbull."

Webster himself penned most of the material in *The American Magazine;* it was his desire to make it a learned magazine, filled with ideas, information, and argument. His interest in language showed clearly in the publication, and he did his best writing when he took up the subject of language.

Webster also continued to write on the new Constitution, but his offerings do not compare favorably with the papers by Hamilton, Madison, and John Jay collected under the title of *The Federalist*. Noah opposed perpetual freedom of the press, fearing that the principle would be abused. His position doesn't seem so surprising for an editor or even a first-rate political scientist, if considered in the context of the state of journalism in the 1780s. There were virtually no libel laws in those days, and many of the more scurrilous publications printed scandal, libel, and even dirty jokes. Webster also repeated his convictions that civil power rested in property, prompting him to argue against a Bill of Rights on the ground that a general distribution of property in America was better insurance for civil liberties than any legal or constitutional guarantees. He sarcastically noted that if the new Constitution had to have such rights, one should be "that Congress shall never restrain any inhabitant of America from eating and drinking, at seasonable times, or prevent his lying on his left side, in a long winter's night, or even on his back, when he is fatigued by lying on his right."

In his writings on government, Webster first fell directly afoul of Thomas Jefferson, for he interpreted Jefferson's writings against altering the Virginia Constitution as indication that he also opposed ever changing the new federal Constitution. Jefferson claimed that he had been misinterpreted, but Webster refused to stand corrected, a stubbornness that would have repercussions for much of the rest of his life.

If *The Federalist* overshadows the articles on government in *The American Magazine*, Webster's sketches, defense of the new Constitution, and other writings still have the ring of a sophisticated political scientist possessed of twentieth-century knowledge and background. Overall, he continued to help create a climate of opinion that led to the eventual ratification of the Constitution. (The old Articles of Confederation Congress arranged for its own demise by ordering national elections for January 1789.)

The American Magazine proved more exceptional because of Webster's comments and suggestions on education, many of which he adopted or adapted from a plan for a national system of education proposed by Dr. Rush in 1786. Noah urged universal public education, at this time possible only in New England. The object, he said, should be to diffuse knowledge of the arts and sciences and "to implant in the minds of the American youth, the principles of virtue and liberty, and inspire them with just and liberal ideas of government, and with an inviolable attachment to their own country."

"When I speak of diffusion of knowledge," he explained, "I do not mean merely a knowledge of spelling books and the New Testament. An acquaintance with ethics and with the general principles of law, commerce, money and government, is necessary for the yeomanry of a republican state." To these subjects he added: "A selection of essays, respecting the settlement and geography of America: the history of the late revolution and of the most remarkable characters and events that distinguished it, and a compendium of the principles of the federal and provincial governments, should be the principal school book in the United States."

Noah wanted children to absorb and formulate ideas in their educational experience, so he objected to the dull rote method of learning and the time wasted in learning subjects, such as Latin and Greek, that would never have practical value. From his brief experience teaching mathematics in Philadelphia at the Episcopal Academy he had decided that math should not be introduced too soon to children.

Finally, he advocated that the value of a virtuous life be taught students.

For this reason society requires that the education of youth should be watched with the most scrupulous attention. Education, in a great measure, forms the moral characters of men and morals are the basis of government. Education should therefore be the first care of a legislature; not merely the institution of schools, but the furnishing of them with the best men for teachers. A good system of education should be the first article in the code of political regulations; for it is much easier to introduce and establish an effectual system for preserving morals, than to correct by penal statutes the ill effects of a bad system.

Webster advocated that elementary education be conducted for at least four months each year "when boys are not otherwise employed." He also urged provisions for teaching teachers and prospective teachers to instruct more effectively.

In his magazine, Webster conducted other campaigns as well
—for copyright and patent laws, for further public awareness of
American history. In order to assist in the latter, he published
abridgments of Captain John Smith's *History of Virginia* and William
Roberts' *History of Florida,* and asked his readers to assist him with
their recollections and documents.

The editor solicited articles from Jeremy Belknap, a Congregational clergyman in Boston who wrote *The History of New Hampshire*
and other historical works. He also tried to interest Belknap's
friend, Ebenezer Hazard, who later was to become postmaster
general, to write for him. The two carried on a backbiting correspondence about Webster. Hazard in 1788 wrote to Belknap, "He
certainly does not want understanding, and yet there is a mixture
of self-sufficiency, all-sufficiency and at the same time a degree of
insufficiency about him which is [to me] intolerable."

They referred to him as "No-ur Webstur esquier junier cri-
tick" and "coxcomb general of the United States."

Belknap at one point wrote to Hazard:

> I find myself under some embarrassment with regard to this personage
> [Webster]. However, as he is going to marry into a family [the Greenleafs]
> with some branches of which I have long had a very agreeable connection, I
> must suffer myself to be in a Degree of acquaintance with him, especially if
> (as he threatens) he should make this place [Boston] his future residence. If
> I cannot esteem him as a friend, I do not wish him an enemy, and I am very
> awkward in the art of Chesterfield.

While editing the magazine, Webster took a leading role in
founding the Philological Society "for the particular purpose of
ascertaining and improving the American tongue." After much
cajoling he secured the society's endorsement of his speller, but it
withheld approval of the grammar, which it deemed radical.

Members contributed verse, plays, and learned discourses.
One of the group, William Dunlap, a dramatist, portrait painter,
and historian, wrote a bad satire that gives a good idea of how some
contemporaries saw Webster:

> What a curst boring fellow now that is,
> You may read Pedant in his very phiz,
> By Mars I swear and by the major-ship
> His very looks give gentlemen the hip.

In another farce, Webster is depicted as the schoolmaster of old dunces:

> When first I join'd them how oft did I hammer
> Night after Night, to teach the dunces Grammar.
> My Rules, my lectures, ev'ry night repeated
> Began to talk sometimes ere they were seated
> To shew my zeal I ev'ry night held forth
> And deep imprest th' idea of my worth
> Not soon forgot.

With arguments drawn from the bibliography of recorded history, Webster bored his Philological Society listeners and probably his readers, too, because his subscription lists fell off. He pontificated before both forums. When he argued before the society, he grew red in the face with the moral earnestness of a Puritan preacher. His fierce sarcasm lacked Franklin's good humor or others' rollicking fun or wit. Eventually both his readers and listeners grew weary of his harangues, and he disbanded his magazine in late 1788, having lost 250 pounds on the project.

On his 30th birthday in 1788, Webster lamented: "30 years of my life gone—a large portion of the ordinary age of man! I have read much, written much, and tried to do much good, but with little advantage to myself. I will now leave writing and do more lucrative business. My moral conduct stands fair with the world, and, what is more, with my own Conscience. But I am a bachelor and want the happiness of a friend whose interest and feeling should be mine."

Although a commercial failure, the magazine had proved to Webster that he could edit a periodical. He tried unsuccessfully to interest Belknap, Hazard, and others in jointly sponsoring an historical magazine that he proposed to call *The United States Register.* When this came to nothing, he returned to visit his parents in Hartford, then went on to Boston to visit Rebecca and put to press a revised version of his lectures, *Dissertations on the English Language.*

Isaiah Thomas printed the book in lieu of royalties on the *Institute.* It was the most handsomely printed volume yet to appear under the Webster by-line. Noah described his book as

full of criticisms, which some will call good sense and others nonsense. People who will take the trouble to read it will say I have a
wonderful knack at finding faults where they before found beauties. I shall
assert some strange things; some of them will be proved; and others, the
world will say, are left unsupported. Men who are friendly will be inclined
to believe me; those who know nothing and care nothing about me will
care as little about my writings; and a host of adversaries, whose favorite
authors I attack, will kick and flounce til they fall themselves or throw me.
Apropos: Some great men with whose works I have taken liberties stand
with their mouths open, ready to devour the child as soon as it is born.
But an author's brats are doomed to be the sport of a mad world; I have
treated others as I thought they deserved; and probably mine will fare as
well.

An octavo volume of 410 pages appeared in May 1789. It
contained the five dissertations on language delivered during the
lecture tour, with copious notes and an appendix that attempted to
promote spelling reforms.

Dr. Stiles thanked him for a gift of a copy to the Yale College
Library: "We glory in a son of this Alma Mater that can be the
author of such a learned production." And *The Massachusetts Magazine* praised "the depth of philological knowledge, justness of sentiment, and purity of style."

The book did combine sense and nonsense, as its author had
predicted. The nonsense included strident attacks on Dr. Samuel
Johnson and others and some wrongheaded theories on philology,
based on Horne Tooke's ideas. Even so, Webster's etymological
opinions were not nearly so wrong as those put forward by Johnson.
The study of comparative philology had barely begun at this time,
and Webster put himself into the lead of students in the field with
this book.

Webster espoused one interesting theory on the circumstances
which "render a future separation of the American tongue from the
English necessary and unavoidable":

The vicinity of the European nations, with the uninterrupted com-
munication in peace and the changes of domination in war, are gradually
assimilating their respective languages. The English with others is suffering continual alterations. America, placed at a distance from those nations,
will feel in a much less degree, the influence of the assimilating causes; at
the same time, numerous local causes, such as a new country, new associa-
tions of people, new combinations unknown in Europe, will introduce

new words into the American tongue. These causes will produce, in a course of time, a language in North America as different from the future language of England as the Modern Dutch, Spanish, and Swedish are from the German or from one another.

Other Americans, including Jefferson, adopted this theory and found it attractive for nationalistic reasons. As a philologist and linguist, Webster later discarded it as unlikely and even undesirable. Thus, the man who first introduced the theory gave rise to an idea that would come to haunt him. For a century warfare raged over the notion, with Webster as the focal point because he had written both for and later against it.

Opponents accused him of vacillation and even deliberately changing his opinions to generate publicity. Not at all, replied Webster. "I have frequently changed my mind as new facts come to light or new arguments indicate a different course."

He wrote his introduction to the *Dissertations* in simplified spelling, arousing much ridicule. The reaction was one reason why Webster began to abandon his spelling reforms, although he persisted with some of the reforms for years.

The spelling experiment may also have contributed to the book's poor sales. *Dissertations* lost him money that he could ill afford to lose because he wanted to marry.

The longer Noah remained in Boston and near Becca Greenleaf, the more he wanted to marry her. Her brother, James, had supported his cause with the family, but at the same time he urged the impatient suitor to wait until his finances had improved.

Webster decided that the law offered the best chance for improvement, but he believed it wiser to practice in Hartford where he was known than in Boston where he remained relatively unknown.

Accordingly, Noah went back to his birthplace, where he enjoyed modest success. That, plus his prospects for royalties from his books, which could reasonably bring him 200 to 300 pounds per year, seemed enough on which he and his bride could live. In June 1789 he wrote to James:

I think it prudent and best to marry as soon as a house can be obtained and furnished. For this we can depend wholly on your goodness; and the sooner you can make it convenient to assist your sister, the sooner you will make us happy. We have habits of economy and industry; but we are perhaps more ambitious to be good than great. It gives me some pain that Becca will have to leave her friends,—friends which can no where be replaced. But no consideration can separate us, and she will cheerfully go where my interest leads me. For this, she is entitled to my warmest gratitude; indeed, I hardly know which she has the most of, my gratitude or my love.

The prosperous James gave Webster an order for one thousand dollars with which to buy furniture. Becca spent it with more taste than economy and ended up with no money for the "best room," the kitchen, or her clothes. Webster had to supply the deficiency.

Noah and Rebecca were married on October 26, 1789, in her father's home in Boston. She was 23, eight years younger than the groom. In his diary he noted:

This day I became a husband. I have lived a long time a bachelor, something more than thirty-one years. But I had no person to form a plan for me in early life and direct me to a profession. I had an enterprising turn of mind, was bold, vain, inexperienced. I have made some unsuccessful attempts, but on the whole have done as well as most men of my years. I begin a profession at a late period of life, but have some advantages of travelling and observation. I am united to an amiable woman, and, if I am not happy, shall be much disappointed.

Chapter 12

THE HARTFORD DETOUR

On Thanksgiving Day in 1789 the newlyweds visited Noah's parents. Little children of the family crowded around the new aunt and marveled at her elegant manners and her dress of thick green brocade, flowered with pink and red roses.

But the mother-in-law wept when she saw her. Becca was so tiny, so unlike her own tall daughters and so different from most girls around West Hartford.

The new Mrs. Webster's social introduction to the rest of Hartford was delayed because she came down with a bad case of the flu almost immediately upon her arrival in her new house, a house that was much more spacious than her in-laws' home. Her illness, plus her knowledge that she had strained her husband's slender resources with her extravagant furnishings, cast a pall on the early days of their marriage.

Yet Rebecca shared her husband's ebullient spirits, and she soon began entertaining on an almost lavish scale. She wrote to brother James that at one party she served as hostess to

a large company of the most respectable citizens . . . on my left hand sat the Hon. Jesse Root, (chief justice of Connecticut); John Trumbull, author of M'Fingal; Peter Colt, Esq., Treasurer of this state; Ralph Pomeroy, Esq., Comptroller General; Enoch Perkins, Esq., an Attorney at Law; James Watson, Esq. . . . if we unite to the above names that of Noah, Priscilla [Becca's sister who was visiting her] and Rebecca, I think they will make a notable appearance for one table—but I forgot to mention the Hon. Jeremiah Wadsworth, who was one of the company.

So sumptuous a beginning of married life drew this comment from Trumbull: "Webster has returned and brought with him a very pretty wife. I wish him success, but I doubt in the present decay of business in our profession whether his profits will enable him to keep up the style he sets out with. I fear he will breakfast upon Institutes, dine upon Dissertations, and go to bed supperless."

Although the Websters stayed in Hartford nearly four years, Trumbull's forecast proved to be uncomfortably close to the truth. However, the dearth of legal business gave the new husband plenty of time for other activities, of which he had many.

Writing, of course, took up the major portion of Noah's spare time. Even if he had been busy with legal affairs, he would not have stopped the pursuit that had become almost as necessary to him as breathing. His most interesting venture was a series of homilies that he published in *The Connecticut Courant* and then in book form. Although these seemed to depart radically from anything he had ever before attempted, he actually wrote the same kind of Poor Richard essays that Ben Franklin had made popular and that he himself used in his speller to illustrate various virtues.

Now he aimed at a more adult level, but his style was so different that even his immediate family didn't know he had authored them. Beginning in December 1790, the homilies appeared in the *Courant* under the pseudonym The Prompter. They proved so successful that other newspapers reprinted them, encouraging Webster to issue them in a book entitled *The Prompter,* first published by Thomas & Andrews in Boston in 1791. As late as 1849, nearly 100 editions had appeared, making it his best seller after the speller. As with the speller, the work gave rise to piracy and plagiarism. Joseph Dennie, an essayist and journalist, patterned his *The Lay Preacher* on *The Prompter.* British printers blatantly pirated it, although American copyright laws offered Webster a little more protection than he had enjoyed during the early days of the speller.

The essays themselves contain humor and gentle satire, in marked contrast to his other writing. Their homely, pithy prose helped influence a generation of American authors, weaning them away from the ponderous style of Johnson and Gibbon. In his preface, Webster wrote, "The writer of this little book took it into his head to prompt the numerous actors upon the great theater of life."

Some of his titles include "Green Wood Will Last Longer than

Dry," "The Fidgets," "The Nose," "Every One to His Notion," "He Would Have His Own Way," "If I was He," "He is Sowing His Wild Oats," and "The Grace of God in Dollars." Here is the last mentioned in its entirety:

> I met a fat plump faced speculator the other day, staggering under a heavy canvass bag. With true Yankee freedom, I asked him what he had in his bag. "The Grace of God," replied the wag. "Ah," said I, "I have often heard of that article, but never saw it in a bag." By this time he had flipped his hand into the bag, and taking out a dollar, "There," said he "Dei Gratia Carolus III is stamped upon the face of every dollar in the bag." I was surprised to hear a speculator say he had the grace of God, especially such a God as to stagger under it; but upon explaining himself, my surprise ceased & I smiled. He had cleared three hundred dollars that morning, by the sale of publick paper—He was too much pleased with the abundance of his grace to stand difficult nice points—& we parted.

Webster continued to look upon himself as a prompter, urging people to correct thoughts and actions. However, some others often saw him as an irritating busybody, poking into a myriad of subjects that need not concern him.

The range of Webster's interests and activities during the four years he and Becca spent in Hartford suggests a man almost frantic to find himself.

First, Noah became a determined clubman despite his lone-wolf temperament. He joined the Hartford Wits. The word *wit* was in the eighteenth-century sense of knowledge or wisdom; nothing very funny issued from their meetings. Dr. Lemuel Hopkins struck at political as well as medical quacks. Dr. Mason F. Cogswell wrote oriental tales and Richardsonian letters. Theodore Dwight, brother of Timothy, trumpeted Yankee superiority. And Timothy put his campaign for the presidency of Yale College in their laps, his poetic impulses and even his nationalism sublimated for the moment to his all-consuming personal ambition.

Webster returned to poetry, presenting to the *Courant* and the *Mercury* the traditional newsboys' addresses for 1790, the aim being to persuade subscribers to tip the carriers at the end of the year. The last two lines make the point:

> For boys, like wheels, in constant toil,
> Will lag and creak, without oil.

About this time Noah waxed lyrical about the French Revolution, then in its early, temperate stages:

> Fair Liberty, whose gentle sway
> First blest these shores, has cross'd the sea,
> To visit Gallia and inflame
> Her sons their ancient rights to claim.
> From realm to realm, she still shall fly,
> As lightning shoots across the sky,
> And tyrants her just empire own,
> And at her feet submit their crown.

Webster also wrote on language. He prepared 14 articles for *The American Mercury* "on the corruptions and errors which prevail in the English language." In these articles he asked for uniformity in word meanings throughout the country. For example, he chided Maryland and Virginia for calling their legislatures the "Supreme Judicial Court" instead of reserving the term *court* for its normal meaning. He sought to eliminate erroneous or ambiguous expressions, such as "more inconsiderable" and to advocate idioms like "Who did he see?" and "them horses."

In these articles he still flirted with spelling reforms:

Them is properly in the nominativ as well as the objectiv. The people at large, who are seldom without the warrant of antiquity, say *them horses* are sold, or he has sold *them horses.* These expressions may be censured as vulgar, but I deny that they are ungrammatical. As far as records extend, we have positiv proof that these phrases were originally correct. They are not vulgar corruptions; they are as old as the language we speak, and nine-tenths of the people still use them. In the name of common sense and reason, let me ask what other warrant can be produced for *any* phrase in *any* language? Rules as we call them, are all formed on *established practice* and on nothing else.

Webster's critics thought they could cut him to ribbons as a result of his articles and his book *Dissertations.* He replied to the critics in his last article:

Much censure has been thrown upon the writer of these remarks by those who do not comprehend his design, for attempting to make innovations in our language. *His vanity prompts him to undertake something new,* is the constant remark of splenetic and ill-natured people. But any person who will read my publications with a tolerable share of candor and attention, will be convinced that my principal aim has been to check *innovations,* and bring back the language to its purity and original simplicity.

Some of the criticism against him resulted from his publication in June 1790, of *A Collection of Essays and Fugitiv Writings,* articles written for newspapers during the lecture tour and articles taken from *The American Magazine.* In this, he used simplified spelling more extensively than he had in anything else he had yet published in book form. The spelling drew much more comment than the ideas expressed, much to Webster's chagrin, and, furthermore, the book lost money.

In the same year, a financially embarrassed Webster published still another book that lost him money, Governor John Winthrop's *Journal.* This source book on colonial history has aided countless students, teachers, and historians, thanks to Webster's generosity in getting it into print. Nowhere in the original edition does his name appear.

As 1791 rolled around, Webster turned his attention to economics. He wrote "On the Utility of Banks," urging the establishment of a bank in every state. He pointed out the "necessity of encouraging home manufactures," in an article that anticipated many of the points and arguments Alexander Hamilton would later make. Other articles that he wrote under the pen name of "Patriot" appeared in the *Courant* throughout 1791 and into 1792. They suggested ways that Hartford could improve its economic prospects, including the establishment of a bank. Webster argued so persuasively that the Hartford Bank was established in 1792. He, John Trumbull, and Chauncey Goodrich prepared and presented to the Connecticut Legislature a petition asking for incorporation. Ironically, Webster couldn't afford to buy a single share of stock in the institution—unfortunate because the bank flourishes to this day under a slightly modified name.

As a result of all this activity, he was nominated for the Hartford Common Council, elected in 1792, and reelected in 1793. Thus, he entered politics at the lowest rung on the ladder. Trumbull and Goodrich had started at this level, too, the former having already risen to the office of district attorney and soon to become a judge, and the latter soon to become a congressman.

Webster promptly made his presence felt. He began an investigation of Hartford records to determine encroachments upon city property by private individuals, and he won a return to the city of valuable riverside land. He instituted ordinances to build new gutters, canals, and streets. Some roads were paved, a rarity in those days. Although most of his writings dealt with abstract or theoretical subjects, he concentrated on homely projects as a practicing politician.

Webster also agitated for a charitable society, arguing for a form of unemployment insurance—the first written proposal for such insurance in the United States, as far as can be determined.

Webster was also active in founding one of the nation's first abolitionist societies, the Connecticut Society for the Promotion of Freedom and the Relief of Persons Holden in Bondage. In his *Effects of Slavery on Morals and Industry,* written in 1793, he concerned himself with the harmful economic and social effects of the "peculiar institution," not with its offenses against mankind. His gradualist approach to emancipation and his preoccupation with the dollars-and-cents aspects of freeing the slaves, suggests that Noah was not motivated by entirely humanitarian sympathies.

Noah wrote often, usually in the *Courant,* about the French Revolution. He upheld the rights of the French citizens to revolt against oppressors, but he grew increasingly alarmed at their excesses. He saw parallels with Shays' Rebellion and joined with Trumbull and Goodrich in writing an "Address from the Inhabitants of Hartford to the President of the United States." They supported Washington and his Proclamation of Neutrality of April 22, 1793, concerning the war between the French and English. Washington probably appreciated their support because he got little for this policy elsewhere.

Webster also concerned himself with mail robberies. Timothy Pickering, the postmaster general, commissioned Noah to try a plan he had suggested of marking and inspecting letters, then tracing them through the post offices. The thief, working in the New York office, learned of the scheme and evaded detection for two years. By this service, Noah may have been the first postal inspector in the United States.

In his small garden, Webster experimented with soils, fertilizers, and seeds. He recorded meteorological data. He investigated dew and its effects on soil, wood, brick walls, and wet and dry cellars. An epidemic of smallpox broke out in Hartford in 1792, and he led the Town Council in authorizing physicians to inoculate willing subjects. In the spring of 1793, his children came down with scarlet fever. Characteristically, he investigated all known references to the disease. Although the girls recovered, he never forgot the experience or his researches and would later put it to use—in, of course, a book.

Despite his many activities in Hartford, Webster found himself increasingly in debt. He couldn't earn enough from law to support his growing family. His first child, Emily Scholten Webster (named in honor of the family into which brother-in-law James had married in Amsterdam) was born August 4, 1790. A second child and daughter, Frances Juliana (always called Julia), was born February 5, 1793.

By July 1793, his debts still held at $1,815, losses from the *Dissertations* and the Winthrop *Journal* coming on top of the sum he still owed for his college expenses and lecture tour. This total did not include the loans from James Greenleaf because they had by then become gifts.

Webster did have assets—$680 in debts owed him, a law library worth $300, and his copyright for which he had been offered $1,250. He again asked James Greenleaf, who had returned to the United States, for advice: "All I ask (or ever wished)," he wrote on June 24, 1793,

is business and whether on a large or small scale, I will be satisfied with it. To renounce all my literary pursuits, which are now very congenial with my habits, would not be altogether agreeable; but it would not make me unhappy. There are many pleasures in agriculture, and if our plan for book-selling upon a pretty large scale should fail, my second wish would be a farm. A man with a just mind and moderate talents may be respectable in almost any department of business.

Like most people who have never pursued business, he underestimated its difficulties and demands. He had been tempted by a proposal, suggested by Dr. Nathaniel W. Appleton who had married Sally Greenleaf, to go into parnership with Childs, the Boston publisher, or take over the Boston Book Store. But Mrs. Webster turned down these projects because she feared she could not live as well as her sisters.

Brother-in-law James finally came up with a proposal, that Webster start a newspaper in New York City. Alexander Hamilton, Rufus King, John Jay, and other Washington supporters wanted a good Federalist paper and would put up money to get it started. John Fenno edited a Federalist paper, *Gazette of the United States,* but he had moved it to Philadelphia. Furthermore, he had trouble competing journalistically with the Jeffersonians, now increasingly vocal as party lines jelled. In New York, the Jeffersonians had Thomas Greenleaf (no relation to the Boston Greenleafs), publisher of the *New-York Journal.*

In August Webster consulted with the principals, agreeing to form a partnership with George Bunce to create a printing company. In November, he moved to New York, to start *The American Minerva.*

He hated to leave Hartford, where he had made his political and literary, if not financial, marks. Furthermore, his mother was dying. Yet his financial needs were so pressing that he had little choice.

In addition, his taste for politics was whetted by his local experiences in Hartford. He yearned to test the political waters on a national scale.

Federal politics had heated up considerably since Washington's unanimous and unopposed election as the first president in 1789.

Although Washington left financial and most domestic affairs to the brilliant first secretary of the treasury, Alexander Hamilton, he gave his secretary of state, Thomas Jefferson, no such freedom.

The discord and complexity in foreign affairs first showed itself in 1790 when a threatened war between Spain and England offered the United States an opportunity to press American claims against both countries. Although this crisis passed, the general European tensions continued and, with them, a notable increase in the cordiality of European nations toward the United States. England and the United States resumed full diplomatic relations for the first time since the revolution.

When war did break out in 1793 between England and France,

something close to war broke out between Hamilton and Jefferson. Hamilton favored the British, Jefferson the French. Washington favored neutrality and won Hamilton somewhat reluctantly to the same position. Although it may never be proved conclusively, the U. S. secretary of state may have surreptitiously encouraged the French ambassador, Citizen Edmond Genêt.

With Jefferson's likely complaisance, Genêt commissioned American ships to sail as privateers under the French flag; he set up courts to condemn the ships they captured; and he arranged an expedition of western frontiersmen to attack Spanish New Orleans.

This enraged Washington. He accepted Jefferson's resignation, effective as of the end of 1793, and he looked for verifiable incidents he could use to demand Genêt's recall. Noah Webster could testify to one such incident. The testimony propelled him with a bang back into journalism as a leading spokesman for Washington, Hamilton, and the Federalists.

Chapter 13

THE FEDERALIST WAY

On August 12, 1793, Noah Webster arrived in New York to iron out details of his proposed new venture. He picked his way through an unruly crowd to his lodgings at Bradley's Tavern in Maiden Lane. It was Citizen Genêt, the consul general from France, who had attracted the mob. The lively, heavyset Frenchman was staying at the same place as Noah.

Genêt drew attention everywhere he went in the United States —whether it was Charleston, South Carolina, or Philadelphia, or New York. He spoke excellent, but charmingly accented English, and used his nation's emotional claims on Americans plus his personality and self-assurance to try to push the young country onto the French side during the French-English wars. Jefferson seemed to have supported him. Jacobin Clubs springing up in many areas of the nation openly urged President Washington to support the ally that had helped him win the Revolution. But Washington saw this as disastrous for America and gave no encouragement.

The frustrated Genêt had begun to snarl undiplomatic remarks about the president, vice president, and the United States by the time he reached New York City. Thomas Jefferson had probably stirred up the mob that greeted him there. Although no doubt Jefferson would never have written such an inelegant line himself, he approved of an attack on John Adams by someone calling himself "Wigwam," who wrote in Greenleaf's *New-York Journal:* "Was he to embrace a stinking prostitute, and endeavor to palm her on the people of America for an unspotted virgin, he would not, in my opinion, act a more infamous part than he has done."

Webster dined with Genêt and his party that night, drew them out, and goaded the minister to such a fury that he blurted that the "officers of our government were in the British interest." One member said something in French to Genêt, thinking Webster could not understand. But Webster did and immediately informed Oliver Wolcott by letter. Wolcott was an ardent Federalist who would succeed Hamilton as secretary of the treasury. He and Webster had been roommates for a time at Yale and remained friends for nearly 60 years. Wolcott passed along the letter to Hamilton and Washington. The president asked for an affidavit. Webster testified that Genêt claimed President Washington, by his actions, was making war against the French and that the "Executive of the United States was under the influence of British Gold." Webster also trapped Genêt by asking him if he believed "our Executive Officers, the President, Mr. Jefferson, Mr. Hamilton and General Knox [Secretary of War] to be fools." The French minister replied, "Mr. Jefferson is no fool."

This was enough to demand that Genêt be recalled. But the ex-minister was too wise to return to turbulent France. He chose instead to marry Governor Clinton's daughter and to settle down on Long Island. With her money he became a gentleman farmer.

As a result of this episode, Noah had no trouble finding backers for his new paper. A group of Federalists including John Jay, Rufus King (U. S. senator from New York and later U. S. minister to Great Britain), James Watson (Federalist leader in New York City and a Yale graduate, class of 1776), James Greenleaf, Alexander Hamilton, and several others, put up $150 each—loans that were all repaid.

The first issue of *The American Minerva* appeared on December 9, 1793, to be published daily except Sunday. A sister paper, the semiweekly *Herald,* was published along with it. This second newspaper was the first weekly semiweekly, or triweekly paper in the United States designed for circulation throughout the country, and made up without recomposition. Thus, Webster pioneered a trend in newspaper publishing that lasted until the midnineteenth century when the coming of the telegraph made the practice unnecessary.

For the first two years of the newspapers' existence, the entire editorial and business management fell on Webster alone.

In the first issue of the *Minerva* he wrote:

In no country on earth, not even Great Britain, are newspapers so generally circulated among the body of the people as in America. To this facility of spreading knowledge over our country, may, in a great degree be attributed, to that civility of manners, that love of peace and good order and that propriety of public conduct, which characterizes the substantial body of citizens in the U. S.. . . . But newspapers are not only vehicles of what is called news; they are common instruments of social intercourse, by which the citizens of this vast republic constantly discourse and debate with each other on subjects of public concern.

From 1793 to 1798, Webster promoted the policies of the Washington administration—notably neutrality. Although others considered him a spokesman for such leading Federalists as Jay and Hamilton, he considered himself nonpartisan and constructive. He was affronted when enemies claimed he was "in the pay" of the Federalists. Even if he were (which is doubtful), they paid him badly because he frequently found himself in financial straits with the papers.

In his two publications, Webster contributed much to making George Washington a symbol of Americanism. He wrote one of the first comprehensive histories of the Revolutionary War, which appeared in his columns. He gave wide circulation to the speeches of Revolutionary thinkers, and otherwise helped to build a nucleus of American folklore on which he and others could begin to elaborate a sense of American nationhood.

Webster capitalized on a lingering hostility toward the British to accomplish his ends, and at times he took advantage of American ignorance of Europe to caricature and attack its manners and morals. He accentuated the positive by extolling the future glory of America.

Besides promoting Americanism in language, education, manners, and politics, Webster proposed unemployment insurance, city planning, cleaning the city streets, improving penal laws, investigating diseases, collecting statistics, forest conservation, organizing charitable enterprises, and the government's purchase and freeing of slaves.

He wrote a history of commerce and the first pages toward a history of epidemics. No newspaper of that era reported so fully on America's move toward complete independence nor offered so many ways to attain it. In addition to all this, he found time to develop a fuel-saving fireplace.

Above all, Webster preached that America should stand on its own feet and never accept the hegemony of England, France, or any other nation. He wrote for the newspaper more than enough material to fill 20 volumes. This does not include the hundreds of columns he translated from French newspapers. From foreign correspondents, such as the learned German historian Christopher Daniel Ebeling, or from Americans such as Jay, King, and Ellsworth when they visited Europe, he presented the best coverage of events abroad available in America.

Webster wrote most often on the French Revolution. His descriptions of the Reign of Terror did much to cool Americans' sentimental ardor for the French cause.

He performed another notable public service by supporting the treaty with Great Britain negotiated by John Jay. Jefferson and the powerful Jacobin Clubs began opposing Jay and his efforts even before the chief justice had reached Great Britain. Writing under the pen name of Curtius, Noah asked for a delay in judgment until Jay had completed his mission.

The treaty provided that northwest posts should be evacuated by the British by June 1, 1796, that commissioners should be appointed to settle the northeast and northwest boundaries, and that the claims of British merchants as well as the U. S. claims for compensation for illegal seizures should be referred to commissioners. The remaining articles in the treaty concerned commerce between the two nations.

Rufus King told Jay that "the papers of 'Curtius' had operated more powerfully than any other publication in calming the public mind and restoring confidence in the administration, being from their style and structure peculiarly adapted to the comprehension of the great body of the people."

Jefferson wrote to Madison, "I gave a copy or two, by way of experiment, to honest, sound-hearted men of common understanding, and they were not able to parry the sophistry of Curtius. I have ceased, therefore, to give them. . . . For God's sake, take up your pen and give a fundamental reply to Curtius. . . ."

The "fundamental replies" came from the Jeffersonian editors, Thomas Greenleaf and Benjamin Franklin Bache, who wrote columns of abuse about Webster but didn't rebut his arguments. They referred to him as "most learned Styltus," "self-exalted pedagogue," "rancorous," "base and uncandid," "utter enemy of the

rights and privileges of the people," "quack," "mortal and incura-
ble lunatic," "dunghill cock of faction." They derisively called him
"the sapient editor of the immaculate paper."

Webster never resorted to such tactics in his own papers. He
uplifted the low quality of journalism that then prevailed.

Two examples contrast the tone of Webster, considered the
prime journalistic champion of Federalism, and Bache, the arch-
Jeffersonian writer. When Jefferson, whom Webster disliked and
distrusted, became vice president under John Adams, the editor
wrote:

> Nor can we omit to express a firm hope and belief that the choice of
> Thomas Jefferson to the second place in the government will be produc-
> tive of the most salutary consequences. His attachment to his own country
> and to its honor and independence is universally acknowledged; nor can
> it be believed that any undue preference for a foreign nation will lead him
> to sacrifice the peace, the interest and the happiness of his own. . . .

When Washington retired as president, Bache penned this
gleeful commentary that is tame by comparison with what he had
written about the great general when he was the chief executive:
"If there ever was a period for rejoicing this is the moment—every
heart, in unison with the freedom and happiness of the people
ought to beat high with exultation, that the name of Washington
from this day ceases to give a currency to political iniquity, and to
legalize corruption. . . ."

And Webster developed still another valuable journalistic skill
—accurate prophecy. In 1794 he predicted that "the combined
powers would never conquer France," a prediction fulfilled soon
by the withdrawal of Prussia and Spain from the coalition. He
declared that Robespierre's head would fall under the guillotine
just as Danton's had. On July 4, 1797, he foresaw the arrival in
France of "some popular man who can attract around him a military
superiority." Sure enough, Napoleon Bonaparte soon came along.

When asked how he made such forecasts, Webster answered:
"The exact fulfillment of the prediction indicates nothing more
than an ordinary share of historical knowledge, united with a can-
did comparison of all the circumstances and events. . . ."

The Boston News Letter, published by John Campbell in 1704, was the first American newspaper. Campbell was also the Boston postmaster and took advantage of his position to distribute his sheet. Actually this was a public service at the time, and the postmasters of other towns eventually came to do the same thing. But Webster took the lead in stopping the practice, because it was widely abused by his time. Most postmasters were also tavern keepers who allowed their patrons to read the papers before they reached the subscribers, if they ever reached them at all.

The first daily paper in America was the *American Daily Advertiser,* founded in Philadelphia in 1784. The second was the *Daily Advertiser,* founded in New York in 1785. Webster changed the name of his *Minerva* to *The Commercial Advertiser* in 1797, apparently to take advantage of the lingering support for the now defunct *Daily Advertiser.* He also changed the name of the nationally circulating *Herald* to the *New York Spectator* at the same time.

Statistics on the number of newspapers in the United States at this time are hard to come by, because newspaper proprietors feared that they would be taxed, as in England, if government officials ever learned how many there were. By 1803, the United States probably boasted about 200 papers, at least 17 of which were daily, seven appearing three times a week, 30 appearing twice a week, and 146 once a week.

All newspapers in the 1790s and early nineteenth century were single folded sheets. The reason for this was, that full postage was charged by the sheet, no matter what size, and not by the weight.

The word *museum* was a common newspaper name then, because the word served as a synonym for what we now call *magazine.* Magazine at that time meant storehouse, as in powder magazine.

Wealthy men or people trying to sell a point of view subsidized many newspapers in the 1790s. While advertising did appear in the columns, it didn't begin to support the average publication. Furthermore, much of the advertising was "in house"—that is, inserted by the owner or editor. Webster, for example, commonly advertised his books, particularly the speller, in his papers. This left subscribers as the avenue for most self-support. As Webster was to learn, and as most periodical publishers know to this day, subscription income rarely supports fully a newspaper or magazine. This left many of the nation's newspapers vulnerable to a sponsor's control.

Webster resisted such control stoutly during his entire editorial
career. Indeed, he later fought with one of his backers, Alexander
Hamilton, over his morals and his refusal to support John Adams
as president. As a result, Hamilton sponsored a rival newspaper that
drove Webster from full-time journalism.

Opposition editors were only part of Webster's troubles as a
journalist. He also suffered from inefficient and dishonest em-
ployees. George Bunce had come into the firm as the printer, but
he turned out such a wretched, ill-printed sheet that the editor fired
him on May 1, 1796. George Folliott Hopkins and Joseph D. Webb
succeeded as partners in the new printing firm of Hopkins, Webb,
and Company. Webb turned out to be dishonest. When he refused
to surrender his contract, Webster and Hopkins dissolved the firm
and set up a new one with Hopkins as publisher.

By October 1, 1797, the two papers had a combined circulation of 1,700, one-third larger than any other New York paper.

Noah Webster almost worked himself to death on his job. His
eyes frequently failed him. One friend described them as "lined
with red ferret." Twice he suffered illnesses from which the doctors
thought he would never recover.

Nor did his private life go smoothly. James Greenleaf had
rented a large house for the Webster family at 168 Queen St., in
New York City. Problems arose because the fun-loving James and
a like-minded friend, Charles Lagarenne, a French dandy and royal-
ist, lived with them. The ménage upset Becca, nor did it please
Noah. A breach inevitably opened that never closed.

In 1796 the Websters moved "to the country at Corlaer's
Hook." Becca much preferred rural life and Noah wanted the
pleasures of a garden. Corlaer's Hook has since become one of the
more squalid quarters of New York City along the East River. But
then it was in the country, and the editor seldom got home before
late at night—after a lonely half-mile walk. At this time the city's
limits to the north did not extend beyond Murray Street. Principal
business streets were Water and Queen (now named Pearl). The
narrow streets were poorly paved or not paved at all. Broad Street
was the main avenue. Upper Wall Street contained the fashionable
residences, including Alexander Hamilton's at the corner of Wall
and Broad.

Not all was gloom, however, for the Websters. Their third
daughter, Harriet, was born at Corlaer's Hook on April 6, 1797.

They continued to see their many friends. James Kent, a member in the New York legislature at this time, visited them most frequently. Another guest was Dr. John W. Francis, a prominent doctor, who later wrote this description of Webster: "He was in person somewhat above the ordinary height, slender, with gray eyes, and a keen aspect; remarkable for neatness in dress and characterized by an erect walk, a broad hat, and a long cue."

By 1798 the party system—Republicans vs. Federalists—had definitely formed, much to Webster's horror. Although others thought him just as much a party man, that is, a Federalist, as anyone else, Webster thought of himself as a patriotic American whose ideas happened to match those of the Federalists. He hated party politics because "to be divided is to be ruined."

His alarm over "the turbulence of the democratic spirit" indicated his strong anti-French views, which began during the Genêt episode in 1793 and grew with his study of the French Revolution. He warned his fellows, "Americans! Be not deluded. In seeking liberty, France has gone beyond her."

Webster tended increasingly to equate the Jeffersonian Republicans with the French Jacobin excesses. Thus he started down the road to political disillusion and oblivion.

On April 1, 1798, Noah left New York for New Haven, giving up active editorship of his newspapers, but continuing as owner and correspondent, particularly in the political area.

In the meantime his relations with Alexander Hamilton steadily deteriorated. Webster, always tending toward prudery, couldn't stomach Hamilton's affair with the notorious Mrs. Reynolds. The coup de grace, however, occurred in 1800 when Hamilton wrote in a letter, which was leaked in much the same manner as it could be in the twentieth century, that President John Adams didn't deserve a second term because he did "not possess the talents adapted to the Administration of Government," and because of "extreme egotism and desultoriness of mind."

Webster knew and admired Adams, although he recognized his faults. Noah's brother-in-law, William Cranch, furthermore, was John Adams's nephew. Cranch and Webster at one time thought they were both courting the same Greenleaf daughter, but when they discovered that Noah fancied Becca and William the younger Nancy, they had become firm friends.

Hamilton's letter virtually killed the ailing Federalist Party.

Webster wrote a reply bristling with indignation. He charged Hamilton with "secret enmity," of fomenting schism, of trying to treat secretly with the British, of secretly abetting William Cobbett in assaulting Adams, of "glaring inconsistencies of conduct and indiscretions," and of "ambition, pride and overbearing temper [which] have destined you to be the evil genius of this country."

Hamilton retaliated with his usual indirection. He started a rival newspaper, the *New York Evening Post,* in 1801 and installed William Coleman as editor. Although a hired hand, Coleman had talent. He soon made mincemeat of the *Advertiser,* which had languished under absentee ownership and editorship.

In 1803 Webster finally found a buyer for the paper and retired as editor in favor of Zachariah Lewis, who remained in the job until 1820 when he was succeeded by Col. William L. Stone.

In 1838, when he was 80 years old, Webster made this appraisal of his career as editor and journalist 40 years earlier: "There are many pieces of mine in newspapers, many in New Haven prints, some in Boston ditto, bundles of which are preserved: but none of my writings are worth republishing, unless the Prompter, Grammar, and the Essay on Neutral Commerce may be excepted."

The man who had often been accused of vanity was too modest in this instance. Noah Webster was America's first great newspaper editor. He made technical innovations in plating practices; he helped to improve the distribution of newspapers through the mails; he led all rivals in his foreign coverage; he showed that political commentary could be a journalistic art, not merely puffery; and he perfected the journalistic essay that continues to distinguish good newspapers to this day. Above all, Webster remained his own man and lifted the tone of journalism in the 1790s. Despite the many complaints about twentieth-century journalism, its ethics and competence tower above that of most newspapers at the end of the eighteenth century. Webster began the improvement.

Then, why did he quit the profession? Poor health partly explains his decision. Disappointment about politics and the fall of the Federalists was another reason. But he revealed the underlying reason when he wrote, "I am fatigued with narrating the absurdities of man." Always thin-skinned, Noah Webster grew tired of taking the brickbats of rival editors, weary of the intrigue among his own Federalists, and fatigued of so public a life. Once again, he looked for something else to do.

PART FOUR

Webster the Lexicographer

Chapter 14

WARM-UP FOR THE DICTIONARY

On April 1, 1798, Webster wrote in his diary: "Removed my family to New Haven. My attachment to the State of Connecticut, my acquaintances, my habits, which are literary & do not correspond with the bustl of commerce & the taste of people perpetually inquiring for news and making bargains; together with the cheapness of living, are among my motives for this change of Residence. . . ."

He had left New York with a sense both of relief and failure. In his 40th year, he had at last recognized that scholarship would be his best métier. He planned a scholarly project, a history of epidemic diseases, which he had already begun in New York. It would prove a useful warm-up for his eventual work in lexicography, because it taught him his final lessons in the techniques of literary research so essential in making a dictionary.

Webster's sense of failure arose from a new spirit in the country, a spirit that he could not support—the spirit of democracy then noisily furthered by the clubs and by the party tactics of Jefferson. Ironically, Webster had probably done as much as anyone to foster it. He probably recognized his part in creating this monster, but he could no longer control it.

The genius of Noah Webster's contribution to America's self-image was his recognition that union is built on more than laws and policies, and on economic and political advantages. It is all of these welded by the spirit and symbols of national self-consciousness. He combined in his thought a breadth of concept and interest, as reflected in his phenomenal range of writings, which were all marked by a singleness of purpose. Through all his activities he promoted just one object—creation of a free and unified America. Although his speller and dictionaries are best known, they are only parts of a unifying ideal.

Webster believed that the Jeffersonian Republicans (who later came to call themselves Democrats) disrupted the unity. He never accepted their rebuttal that a sense of nationhood was still possible under a party system because he thought nationalism unlikely without unity. His fears become more understandable when one remembers that the Jeffersonian party made its strongest appeal to the sectional interests of the South. Noah already foresaw—and worried about—the North-South conflict.

Homer D. Babbidge, Jr., comments correctly in his introduction to *Noah Webster: On Being American:*

> In a sense, Noah Webster's career had two distinct acts. The first—and most appealing, from hindsight—was his career as a militant advocate of American union and cultural and political independence. For 15 years, from 1782 to 1797, Webster toiled with enthusiasm and dedication to instill in the hearts and minds of his fellow citizens some of his own passionate love of liberty and to persuade them of the great truth of life, that liberty could be preserved only through the strength that comes of unity. Webster's career as a 'cultural nationalist' entitles him to unchallenged eminence in American life, for his broadly conceived ideal of union and its cultural dimensions surpasses that of his more famous contemporaries.
>
> The second act of Webster's career only partly negated the first. In it, he emerges not so much as an individual proponent of national unity but as a classic symbol of the lost cause of American Federalism. Disillusioned by what he considered the demoralization of American politics, Webster turned, with the century, from political activism to moral criticism, his shining vision of the new America tarnished. With increasing piety and diminishing humanness, Webster moved away from the affairs of men to the pursuits of the mind and the spirit. . . .

Webster's nationalism had two characteristics, remarkable more for their directness and simplicity than for their novelty:

1. Only in union is there sufficient strength to ensure liberty.
2. A sense of nationality is vital to the preservation of unity.

As a corollary to No. 2, he believed that nationality could be best furthered through a common language and culture. His nationalism conspicuously lacked the egalitarian democracy and humanitarianism that characterized French thinking on the subject. Webster, instead, sought to institutionalize liberty. In this he was more a political scientist than a zealot. This cerebral rather than emotional concept of liberty largely accounts for his lack of success in winning many followers. On the other hand, Jefferson took the emotional route and consequently won hero's laurels—some of them undeserved—as one of the giants among the founding fathers. No wonder the two remained at loggerheads throughout their lives.

L. W. Levy in *Jefferson & Civil Liberties,* answers the question of how Jefferson came to have such a reputation as the champion of liberty: "The conventional image of Jefferson was partially fashioned from a national impulse to have a libertarian hero larger than life. When the American people honor Jefferson as freedom's foremost exponent, they reflect their own ideals and aspirations more, perhaps, than they reflect history. . . . Much of his reputation and even influence derived from his habitual repetition of inspired reveries about freedom, expressed in memorable aphorisms."

Webster considered Jefferson his bête noir from 1800 on when the latter defeated John Adams for president. From that year, Noah turned increasingly into the model of the irascible, crotchety conservative, looking with disdain both upon the folly of his youth and its reflections in nineteenth-century democratic practice.

Webster wasn't alone among old-line Federalists in seeing disaster in the Jeffersonian victory. However, while most of them retired into private life, largely abandoning their original confidence in the destiny of America, he never lost his vision. Instead, he funneled his large energies into constructive literary channels.

Webster chose as the setting for his new life the house originally occupied by Benedict Arnold on the then-beautiful shore of New Haven harbor. The location was afterward called Water Street. The house had a center hall; on the right were two spacious rooms; on the left at the front was a second parlor, and behind it the kitchen with a fireplace large enough to take half a cord of wood.

Julia, the second Webster daughter, recalled, "My honored

father's study was over the living room, the east parlor was used as a dining room always. . . . The spacious attic was my play place and the dormer windows my doll's parlor. I remember playing with the scabbard of a sword said to have been Arnold's there."

The first order of business after getting settled was for Webster to investigate the schooling in New Haven. He had been appointed a member of the school visiting committee and didn't like what he found. He called together a group of leading citizens and promptly organized the Union School. He served as treasurer of a company that issued 100 shares of stock. In 1799 the group opened a brick schoolhouse with two rooms, one for boys and one for girls. By 1801 he had become president of the school, which had an enrollment of 52 boys and 63 girls, among them three of his daughters.

Webster did even more for elementary education. He wrote four more textbooks, because the children had little else to study but Latin, arithmetic, Morse's Geography, and his own grammar, speller, and reader. Most of the children had already progressed beyond these, so he framed a series of four new texts under the general title of *Elements of Useful Knowledge.*

The first volume contained a "Historical and Geographical Account of the United States," down to the beginning of the Revolution. Included were Washington's Farewell Address, a condensation of the federal Constitution and of every state constitution, plus a chronology. The second continued the history of the country down to 1789. The third provided "A Historical and Geographical Account of Europe, Asia and Africa." The fourth gave "A History of Animals," and was a simplified textbook on biology. The books appeared, respectively, in 1802, 1804, 1806, and 1812. Although they enjoyed only a short-lived acceptance, they served as the models for many other texts by other authors that followed.

Before entering the Union School, the younger daughters for a time attended the best day school in the neighborhood, taught by Miss Eunice Hall, where they learned to read and write, spell, do arithmetic, and sew. Their attendance ended abruptly with the great eclipse of June 16, 1806. They had been primed, of course, by their learned father to watch the phenomenon that would occur while they were at school. But Miss Hall, out of fear and superstition, refused to allow them to see it.

The enraged Webster withdrew his children at once from the

school, charging that a teacher so ignorant and tyrannical was unfit to instruct his children.

In the meantime, his family had grown, with three more children all born in New Haven. His fourth child and daughter, Mary, was born January 7, 1799. His fifth child and only son who survived infancy, William Greenleaf, was born on September 15, 1801. The sixth child and fifth daughter, Eliza Steele, entered the world on December 21, 1805.

New Haven may have been the prettiest small city in America when the Websters moved there. Rows of elms arched over the streets of the city of 4,000 inhabitants. Wide streets led from the harbor to the Green, or public square, where the State House, the Center Church, and the cemetery reminded the citizens of their obligations. West of the Green stood Yale College. The college always took pride in its alumni, including Webster. Timothy Dwight, who had succeeded in his campaign to become president in 1795, especially welcomed Noah as an ally in the battle to safeguard the established Congregational Church. New Haven was still a stronghold of Federalism, so Noah felt at home among people of congenial political views. Other New Haven citizens cultivated his support to combat legislation hostile to commerce.

The influence and prestige for which Webster had always longed was his in New Haven. Furthermore, he had a large garden in which he could continue with his absorbing horticultural experiments. When fatigued with writing or gardening, he could look across Long Island Sound with Long Island plainly in view on clear days, or see the traffic pass on the Boston Post Road. He and Mrs. Webster were also familiar sights throughout the city on their many strolls—he tall and erect, she tiny and graceful. At this period, walking was their favorite exercise. Webster cut a fine figure in his customary black clothes. He rarely went abroad without his cue, or long cane.

Absentee editorship of his New York papers wasn't nearly enough to keep Noah Webster busy in New Haven. He turned to a project that surprised those who didn't know him. He wrote a history of epidemic diseases—the most exhaustive inquiry ever made until that time into cholera, yellow fever, and other pestilences that had plagued mankind throughout recorded history.

Webster had personally seen epidemics of influenza in 1789

and 1790, and of scarlet fever in April-May 1793, his own children suffering from the latter disease. He wrote about the scarlet fever as though he had been the doctor: "I attended night and day to its symptoms, which were a catarrhal affection of the throat, attended with slight external discoloration about the neck and breast, and a fever whose exacerbations were violent, but the remissions regular, attended with profuse perspiration."

Oliver Wolcott reported to him of the terrible yellow-fever epidemic in Philadelphia in 1793, of the empty streets and the panic. One in every ten who caught the disease died. Total registered deaths reached 4,044 from it. Probably many more unrecorded deaths resulted.

Doctors bickered endlessly about the causes and cures of the pestilences. Some claimed the origins local, some cited imports from abroad. Many thought the plagues a visitation of God to purge foul hearts. Dr. Rush grew so distressed at the theories and countertheories that he withdrew his membership from the prestigious College of Physicians in Philadelphia and organized the Academy of Medicine. Someone obviously not a doctor saw the whole situation this way:

> Doctors raving and disputing,
> Death's pale army still recruiting.
> What a pother,
> One with t'other,
> Some a-writing, some a-shooting.

The doctors began a pamphlet war in which every literate American physician took up his pen. In 1794 epidemics recurred in Philadelphia and appeared fatally in New Haven. New York, Baltimore, and Norfolk were stricken in 1795. Newburyport, Boston, and Charleston suffered bouts in 1796. Webster commented frequently on the epidemics in the *Minerva* and *Commercial Advertiser,* noting "something singular in the appearance and progress of putrid diseases."

He wrote later: "No sober reflecting man can cast his eye over the world, and see the miseries of man, without a humane wish to alleviate them."

As usual, Webster combined this humanitarian motive with his

nationalistic spirit. He saw an opportunity for an American to con-
tribute something that could lead to solutions. His answer was a
written history.

Webster began work on the book in earnest within 10 days of
his moving to New Haven. He quickly found it necessary to ran-
sack the libraries of America—the Loganian in Philadelphia, facilities in New York, Yale's collection, and those at Harvard and in
Boston—for material. But he did more than gather information
from previously published works in libraries. He wrote to all the
prominent men of the time, and he sent out circular letters to
eminent foreign physicians. He interviewed victims of epidemics,
and sea captains and sailors who had encountered pestilences in
their travels. As Dr. Alfred Scott Warthin of the University of
Michigan expresses it, Webster collected "an enormous amount of
material which he arranged systematically and analyzed with that
tireless indefatigability which seems the most remarkable characteristic of this remarkable man."

Although Noah succumbed for 10 weeks with the disease he
was describing, he completed in 18 months, without help, a two-
volume work of 712 octavo pages. His *Brief History of Epidemic and
Pestilential Diseases; with the Principal Phenomena of the Physical World
which Precede and Accompany Them, and Observations Deduced from the
Facts* has the distinction of being the world's first historical treatment of the subject.

Not only did it expertly summarize epidemiological opinion at
the end of the eighteenth century, but it also offered the best
summary of earlier speculations on pestilential disease. The first
volume recounts the diversity of opinions on the causes and origin
of epidemics. The remainder traces the history of epidemics from
Biblical times to 1799. This last section remains invaluable for
medical historians to this day. The second volume presents statistics
and conclusions about the causes of epidemics.

Basically, Webster argued that epidemics occur in certain periods, generally in widely separated places; that a pestilential "state
of air" extends at the same time over many parts of the world; that
violent plagues raging in one part of the world usually mean that
similar pestilences, or at least malignant diseases, will occur elsewhere. He observed that epidemics among humans often are as-
sociated with plagues among animals, earthquakes, volcanic erup-

tions, appearances of comets, and hordes of locusts. But he carefully disclaimed any causal connection between human epidemics and physical phenomena. Being an instinctive scientist, he observed but drew no hard conclusions. But he leaned heavily toward the position that epidemics were electrical in origin. He scoffed at the importation theory and pooh-poohed quarantine measures.

He gloomily concluded: "The pestilence [of deadly epidemic diseases] which invades man will be found to arise solely from the uncontrollable laws of the elements; and quarantine will be utterly unavailing." Quarantines had been attempted at that time, but had failed largely because no one understood the role that rats, fleas, and mosquitos played in bearing the contagion.

While later discoveries have upset Webster's theories, Noah himself knew that his conclusions lacked sufficient data. He inserted this disclaimer: "The reader will consider these opinions rather as *conjectural* than *positive*. No certain conclusions can be drawn from an interrupted and imperfect series of facts. More materials are necessary to enable us to erect a theory of epidemics which shall deserve full confidence." At the end of his history, he proposed "that all medical and philosophical societies [should] undertake to register facts and reciprocally to communicate them by means of general correspondence."

Despite Webster's incorrect theories, his work remains notable. Its pioneering emphasis on statistics and data and its historical approach are its most valuable features.

As usual with Webster's literary efforts, it aroused a storm of controversy. Dr. William Currie, more successful with his pen than with his diagnoses at this time, wrote: "The doctrine of Mr. Webster on this subject, notwithstanding his elaborate researches, appears still more exceptional, and to be as much the creature of the imagination as the tales of the fairies."

Noah's friend, Dr. Rush, had advised him on the manuscript and generally approved of it although the two disagreed about bloodletting. Rush advocated the practice; Webster opposed it and said so with his usual bluntness in the history.

Dr. Joseph Priestley, the philosopher, theologian, and scientist who had been driven from his native England because of radical opinions and who had settled in Northumberland, Pennsylvania, thought Webster deserved "the thanks of all mankind" for "a most important publication."

Although it received, on balance, critical approval, the history failed financially. In this excerpt from an 1801 letter to Dr. Rush, Noah complains:

"I shall never print another [edition of the history]. Not more than 200 copies are sold in this country, and I am 7 or 800 dollars out of pocket on account of it, with all my previous expenses, my labor and toil. I wish physicians in New York and Philadelphia would take the remaining copies, about 700, at a dollar in sheets, the first cost, and distribute them over the country among young students. The young are susceptible of truth; the old are incorrigible."

Although forgotten now, the book was held in high esteem during the nineteenth century and was often pirated. As late as 1832, Webster seriously considered revising and republishing it, but he dropped the idea.

Many doctors ridiculed Webster's history because a layman had written it. The familiar charge of "busybody" came down on his head again. He certainly was a busy body. Besides the history of epidemics and his newspaper-editing duties, he also found time to attempt to compile an almanac. Although numerous publications had already appeared bearing the word *almanac* in their title, no compilation of miscellaneous facts as found in present-day almanacs had yet appeared. Noah sent out on May 7, 1798—only five weeks after he had settled in New Haven and just 27 days after he began the epidemic history—a circular letter requesting statistical information. He asked for such information on geography, health, agriculture, trade, manufactures, shipping, roads, bridges, churches, schools, mines, and "any curious or important information not falling under any of the foregoing heads." He claimed that "I have some leisure and great inclination to be instrumental in bringing forward a correct view of the civil and domestic economy of this State." Not enough replies came in, but Webster never let a good idea die. He made such fact-gathering activity one of the goals of the new Connecticut Academy of Arts and Sciences, which he had played a leading role in organizing. (He continued active in this group until mid-1800, when he stopped attending because of the political sniping against him.)

Another abortive activity resulted from Noah's attempt to write a history of newspapers in America. Not enough editors replied to his circular letter.

But another project bore more fruit, an analysis of culture in America. This arose because of Dr. Priestley's outspoken and uncomplimentary remarks about the state of learning and education in the new nation. Priestley's opinions aroused a storm among the self-conscious Americans, particularly from William Cobbett writing as "Peter Porcupine" in Philadelphia. Although Webster disagreed with Priestley's politics (which were Jeffersonian), he grew even more upset about Cobbett's unfounded claims. Hence, he wrote letters of rebuttal in early 1800.

Webster's letters 9 and 10, especially, give valuable and unusually reliable insight into the state of culture in the United States, or at least in the New England states, at the turn of the century. Notably at variance with the exaggerated claims of America's struggling institutions of higher learning, the letters contain a frank concession of intellectual inferiority by one who would have preferred to give a better report.

Nevertheless, Noah Webster remained confident that the potential for ultimate superiority reposed in the American nation. He restated his conception of education as a function of society. He again stressed the economic foundation for cultural advancement, observing that "science demands leisure and money."

Some of his frank observations about the state of learning are:

"Our colleges are disgracefully destitute of books and philosophical apparatus. . . ."

"I am ashamed to own that scarcely a branch of science can be fully investigated in America for want of books, especially original works."

He points out, however, that

in the eastern states knowledge is more diffused among the laboring people than in any country on the globe. . . . But in the higher branches of literature our learning is superficial to a shameful degree. . . . Perhaps I ought to except the science of law, which, being the road to political life, is probably as well understood as in Great Britain. . . . But as to classical learning, history, civil and ecclesiastical, mathematics, astronomy, chymistry, botany, and natural history—excepting here and there a rare instance of a man who is eminent in some one of these branches—we may be said to have no learning at all, or a mere smattering. And what is more distressing to me, I see every where a disposition to decry the study of ancient and original authors.

Nevertheless, he concludes: "The Americans want only the *means* of improvement—their genius and industry are no where exceeded. . . . Opportunity, means, patronage alone are wanting to raise the character of this country to an eminent rank among nations."

Webster performed one other service during this period, which must rank as another of his lost causes. He became the first writer to decry the spoils system of patronage at the time that it began in Jefferson's administration.

The origins of this battle started with Abraham Bishop, Webster's classmate at Yale, who supported Jefferson and opposed the Federalist and Congregational control in Connecticut. He campaigned actively for Jefferson in the election of 1800. Of course, Noah supported Adams both in his writings and in public speeches.

Of one of Bishop's flaming invectives, Webster wrote: "Much the greatest part is mere rant, declamation and incongruous sentiments, incapable of being comprehended, much less answered. But such parts of the production as are capable of being understood demonstrate the extreme weakness of the writer's head or the wickedness of his heart."

Bishop replied in kind: "As Mr. Webster is very apt to give advice to others, I leave him with a word of advice, which is, to prosecute to conviction and sentence of death the man or men who ever told him that he had talents as a writer."

Yet Bishop really won the last round. His support won for his aged and infirm father, Samuel, Jefferson's appointment to the office of Collector of the Port of New Haven, a lucrative post. To the surprise of no one, Abraham succeeded his father upon the elder Bishop's death two years later.

President Adams had made last-minute appointments before he had turned over the presidency to Jefferson. Jefferson recalled several of these as an invasion of his prerogatives, including the New Haven job that Adams had given to Elizur Goodrich, who was competent and locally popular, but who was a Federalist.

Noah, a friend of Goodrich, wrote a letter of protest to Madison in 1801, asking him to use his influence to prevent further "irritations." Madison passed along the letter to Jefferson for advice on how to deal with it. Jefferson replied: "Tho' I view Webster as a mere pedagogue of very limited understanding and very strong prejudices and party passions, yet as editor of a paper and as of the Newhaven association, he may be worth striking. His letter leaves two very fair points whereon to answer him."

No answer came; so Noah wrote 18 letters, in September 1801, attacking the Jefferson administration, letters which he printed in his newspapers.

Webster charged the president with "hypocrisy and deception," "imbecility and inconsistency," "vanity," "blind confidence," plus an "intolerance despotic, as it is wicked." He ended with this analysis of the spoils system:

Instead of inviting men of sterling integrity to accept places of trust, with the expectation of a permanent support, your practice, by filling our towns with the ghosts of departed officers, will frighten from offices every man of worth, and leave them a prey to the vile and desperate. Instead of giving stability to government by a judicious use of power and distribution of offices, your practice lends a ready support to opposition, feeds the discontented with new hopes from change, and solicits new proselites to faction.

Although Andrew Jackson supposedly invented the spoils system in politics, Jefferson actually started the practice of appointing loyal followers to posts. Webster began attacking the system with Jefferson, and was still doing so in 1832 when Jackson had carried it to its logical extremes. In that year, Noah refused to vote as a symbolic and well-publicized gesture of protest against the spoils system.

Not content to see the letters on the spoils system languish in his newspapers (which suffered from a dwindling circulation), Webster issued them in a pamphlet in 1802, *Miscellaneous Papers on Political and Commercial Subjects*. To this pamphlet he added three other writings, each of which is notable. One was a letter to Rufus King when he served as minister to Great Britain in 1797. In this he "instructed" the envoy on arguments he should use to persuade Britain to stop interfering with American commerce, because the two countries had so many commercial interests in common that they should be partners, not rivals. No evidence exists that King ever made these arguments to the British. If he had done so successfully, the two nations might have avoided the War of 1812.

A second offering was a history of banks and insurance companies in the United States, the first ever written. It presents further evidence that Webster was one of America's best eighteenth-century economists.

The third new writing was the scholarly "Essay on the Rights of Neutral Nations." In it he studied the practices of nations from Greek times to 1800 in support of his doctrine that "free ships make free goods." He argued that the principles of a free commerce should be surrendered only with a nation's independence—a notion that Jefferson implicitly opposed.

If Webster was losing all influence on the national political scene, he retained some influence locally. He was elected common councilman in New Haven in 1799, an office he held for five years; he was appointed justice of the peace annually from 1801 to 1810; he served as justice of the quorum from 1806 to 1810; and the voters sent him to every session of the state legislature between 1800 and 1807. Webster always did his job conscientiously. Yet his stubborness concerning the issues in which he believed antagonized his opponents—and even some of his allies.

For example, his views on property as a basis for the franchise had grown outdated. In arguing in 1802 against a measure before the Connecticut Legislature to abolish property qualifications for voting, he told this anecdote:

> The introduction of this bill reminds me of a circumstance which took place in Philadelphia while Commodore Truston and his crew lay there. The crew were all invited up to Freemen's meeting, their votes were handed them, and they voted according to the wishes of a party. Not long afterwards, when they were returning up the Delaware, from a cruise, they saw a school of Porpoises making towards Philadelphia. One of them asks the other, where are these Porpoises going; why damn it replies the other, to Freemen's meeting to vote for _____.

"I tell this anecdote barely to show the sense which all persons have of the impropriety of admitting persons to vote who have no property or families, to attach them to the interest of the states. . . ." he concluded.

Webster had waved a red flag at a bull. The Jeffersonians in Connecticut began calling themselves porpoises. Bishop picked up the phrase. When Noah tried to explain what he had really meant, he only made matters worse.

This distressed the thin-skinned Webster, who could give out criticism better than he could take it. Although he was forever promising himself and his wife that he would stay out of public fights, he forever found himself in them. The spoils system and porpoise battles proved the last straw—at least for the time being.

The extent of Noah's alarm over almost everything relating to public affairs appears in a cranky and uncharacteristic refusal in 1802—shortly after the Bishop episode—to perform some chore for the Connecticut Academy of Arts and Sciences:

> This is the nineteenth year, since with an ardor bordering on enthusiasm I have been engaged in some kind of service, either wholly or essentially directed to the interest of my country. In this pursuit, which has not always been guided by discretion, I have made many and great sacrifices of my private interest, without the hope or expectation of other reward than the approbation of my fellow citizens. But amidst the turmoil of parties and passions, even this reward is no longer to be expected. Either from the structure of my mind, or from my modes of investigation, I am led very often to differ in opinion from many of my respectable fellow citizens; and difference of opinion is now a crime not easily overlooked or forgiven. The efforts which have been made and are now making to deprive me of the confidence of my fellow citizens, and of course of my influence, and reputation, efforts not limited to this town, render it necessary for me to withdraw myself from every public concern, and confine my attention to private affairs and the education of my children. . . . In the present state of things, my effort can be of little or no use; as I cannot make the sacrifices of opinion, either on matters of science or government which would probably be necessary to command confidence.

This letter came less than a year before he finally disposed of his newspaper, *The Commercial Advertiser,* to Zachariah Lewis in 1803. Lewis found the accounts for the paper in such disarray and the competition from Hamilton's thriving *Post* so formidable that Webster cut his original price of $5,000 to a fraction of that amount. Webster's paper eventually became the *The Globe and Commercial Advertiser,* which died in 1923 when Frank Munsey merged it with the *New York Sun.*

Chapter 15

THE PRELIMINARY DICTIONARIES

One might think that compiling a dictionary is such an obscure and specialized work that the lexicographer himself sinks into oblivion.

Webster thought so and looked forward to escape from so much public attention by losing himself in scholarship. This was not to be, however, and he had himself to blame. He chose to announce his project in the press, and thereby stirred up still another storm. On June 4, 1800, he inserted in New Haven newspapers a typically oblique bit of self-advertising: "Mr. Webster of this city, we understand, is engaged in completing the system for the instruction of youth, which he began in the year 1783. He has in hand a Dictionary of the American Language, a work long since projected, but which other occupations have delayed till this time. The plan contemplated extends to a small Dictionary for schools, one for the counting-house, and a large one for men of science. The first is nearly ready for the press—and the second and third will require some years."

In this, Webster's timing was bad, both because he didn't get the first promised dictionary to press for another six years and because he made his announcement at the same time that his opponents were sniping at his political and medical ideas and his views on language.

The Jeffersonian paper, *Aurora,* pounced on his announcement with glee: "There are some beings whose fate it seems to be to run counter from reason and propriety on all occasions. In every attempt which this oddity of literature [Webster] has made, he appears not only to have made himself ridiculous, but to have rendered what he attempted to elucidate more obscure, and to injure or deface what he has intended to improve. . . . He now proposes to give to the American world no less than three dictionaries!"

That attack was bad enough, but not unexpected. What really hurt were the shafts from his own people, especially from the Boston *Palladium,* voice of New England Federalism and Congregationalism.

Its assistant editor, Warren Dutton, said of Webster in a column he called the "Restorator": "I am willing to allow this gentleman the praise of industry and of good intentions, and sincerely wish I could acquit him of the charges of vanity and presumption. But modesty, most certainly, is not the leading feature in his literary character. . . . But, if he will persist, in spite of common sense, to furnish us with a dictionary which we do not want, in return for his generosity I will furnish him with a title for it. Let then, the projected volume of *foul* and *unclean* things bear his own christian name, and be called Noah's Ark."

Webster replied with a show of good humor, but he never again liked his first name and was to forbid that it weigh down any grandchildren. "Many illiberal remarks have appeared upon my proposed dictionary," he answered. "Whether that work, if ever published, will have merit or not, is a point about which the gentleman may make himself very easy; as it would be as difficult for *me* to *corrupt* and debase the language, as it is for him to *improve* it. If the work should be a real improvement on those before published, my fellow citizens would find it useful, as they have some of my other publications. If not, the loss would rest on myself or the printer, and the work would descend quietly into oblivion, accompanied perhaps by the Restorator."

Webster credited Elizur Goodrich, the man whom Jefferson didn't allow to become the port collector for New Haven, with first suggesting that the schoolmaster-lawyer-editor-reporter-commentator-author compile a dictionary. Goodrich who came from Durham, Connecticut, was a minister and a Yale trustee. However, the genesis of the work came from many sources. As early as 1790, Daniel George, a correspondent from Portland, Maine, wrote: "I was pleased with your useful and approved *Institute:* I admired your learned *Dissertations on the English Language;* but with your late

Collection of Essays and Fugitiv Writings I am pleasingly astonished. Go on, Sir, and make a thoro reform in our orthography. . . . But, Sir, we must first have a Dictionary, and to you we must look for this necessary work."

For many years, Noah had jotted down words he encountered in readings that he had failed to find in dictionaries. His labors upon the speller and the grammar had familiarized him with the problems of defining words and discriminating shades of meaning, and had also disclosed to him the deficiencies in the dictionaries then available.

In large portions of his political and other essays, he defined terms with a care that exasperated his opponents and made even his supporters restless. So well known was his foible that Leonard Chester satirized it in 1801; he put this line into the mouth of a character who was supposed to be John Trumbull: "I believe I must touch up brother Noah—no that won't do either; if he should get angry, he'll oppose my favorite scheme of augmenting the number of judges of the superior court and come into the house and spend three days on the word augmentation."

Noah found the compilation of words congenial and for years collected and categorized facts on every conceivable subject. The ten days that it took him to get settled in New Haven were passed mostly in putting his files in order.

As early as the 1780s, John Adams had bemoaned the lack of an American English dictionary. Many other Americans saw its need, but no one did anything about it—until Webster. By this time, Dr. Samuel Johnson's great dictionary of the 1750s was passé, even in England.

In 1806 Webster finally came out with the first of a series of dictionaries that turned out to be five, not three. He titled the dictionary the *Compendious Dictionary*. In the preface for the 1806 work, Noah commented that becoming self-reliant in language was as vital to American strength as the avoidance of international alliances. He wrote Joel Barlow that American dependence upon English standards was "prejudicial" and had put "an end to inquiry," with the result that even the colleges had "no spirit of investigation."

Thus the making of dictionaries fell readily into the rationale of Webster's whole career. So delighted was he with his newfound project that he even recommended literary pursuits to other vexed and discouraged Federalists. By 1800, at the age of 42, he sensed that he had at last found his true métier in lexicography. Although the 1806 work was not a commercial success and met mixed reviews, Webster, nevertheless, was pleased with it. With his book marketing experience and intuition, he guessed what hurt its sales —its size of 408 pages, plus a 24-page preface set in type smaller than that now used in most metropolitan telephone books. He abridged the 1806 version by cutting its 37,000 words to 30,000 and shortening the definitions. He even managed to reduce the price from $1.50 in 1806 to $1 for the abridgement that appeared in 1807, thus pioneering the inexpensive reference work. The abridgement sold better. Webster would have disposed of many more copies of both versions if he had omitted the preface, in which he rehearsed his linguistic theories and censured Dr. Samuel Johnson unmercifully for his many errors. While it is true that Webster was a better lexicographer than Johnson, he himself should not have made the claim, nor at such length.

Noah called his first dictionary *compendious,* meaning concise. Thousands of the definitions in the 1806 work could be used unchanged in a modern dictionary limited to a vocabulary of the same size. A column-by-column comparison between it and, for, example, *Webster's New Ideal Dictionary,* produced in 1968 in Springfield, Mass., for about the same kind of readership, would confirm the soundness of his definitions.

Yet the *Compendious Dictionary* was not an inflated spelling book for children. It was a meaningful contribution to the development of lexicography prepared for adults. His 37,000-word vocabulary surpassed in size and in correctness the dictionaries then available in London.

For one thing, his work was the first to add technical and scientific terms such as *vaccination, aeriform,* and *electrometer.* He also dared introduce Americanisms such as *skunk, tomahawk,* and *snowshoe.* He even put in legal and political terms such as *selectman, docket, political, presidency, constitutionality,* and *congressional* (an inclusion condemned by critics). He gave lexicographic legitimacy to *cent, dime,* and *dollar* for the first time as units in the American monetary system.

The *Compendious Dictionary* also did more than define words.

It contained tables of money, an official list of all U.S. post offices, census figures on the states, and various chronological tables. Subsequent dictionaries have continued the encyclopedic practice that Webster pioneered.

Although the preface didn't help Webster sell his work, it is noteworthy, nevertheless. Besides the attack on Johnson, it contains a section on orthography in which the author analyzed why it is so difficult to reform spelling, and a section on the even greater difficulties of pronunciation. He also made the practical point that you can't fix a language so that it won't change, as Dr. Samuel Johnson wished to do.

In fact, he understood one of the basic reasons why Johnson's dictionary had failed to survive. It had obsolesced. That is why Webster remained unmoved by criticism that a series of dictionaries was senseless. He knew that by the time he finished each volume in his series the language had changed. New words are coined; words change in meaning; other words disappear.

Webster's recognition of the mutability of language was the result of patient, thorough study. One of the four characteristics that Webster possessed which made him a great lexicographer was his capacity for demanding scholarship. He had studied language, both in the past and in the present. Furthermore, he had the patience of a scholar to continue that study for decades.

A second and related quality lay in Webster's delight in etymological investigation. It was a game to him. He found relaxation in studying languages. He kept his Greek fresh by comparing the English translation of the New Testament with the original. He learned German, Danish, and Anglo-Saxon so he could trace English back to its ancestors. Webster studied Welsh and Old Irish. Old Testament study required Hebrew, so he learned it. Thinking that Hebrew derived from Persian, Noah studied that language as well. Soon he had mastered 20 alphabets from as many languages. He was fascinated by the study of the origin of such a word as *father*. He discovered that the *p* in the Latin *pater* or Greek *patar* became *v* in the German *vater*. That in turn changed to *f* in English.

Some people might say that Webster naturally and intuitively came by his gift for definition, the third quality that made him a great lexicographer. That is perhaps true. But he had cultivated and refined that gift. In every essay he wrote he took time to define with care each important term he used. He hated fuzzy thinking and believed that such thinking lay at the bottom of many of the ills that mankind suffered. He had cultivated a mental precision for years as a writer and speaker. He knew that his lengthy definitions irritated his fellow legislators, but he persisted, nevertheless, because he thought the necessity for a precise meaning transcended the risk of alienating his listeners.

The fourth important quality that made Webster a great lexicographer was the breadth of his knowledge. As a lawyer, he had practiced before local courts, served as legislator and judge, and had written essays and treatises that required deep knowledge of law. He knew more about medicine than many doctors practicing at that time. Science remained a hobby for him all his adult life. As an economist, he ranks among the best in America's early days. Because of his New England inheritance he was a theologian. As a lecturer, schoolmaster, editor, and traveler he had touched life in many ways. Noah Webster had prepared himself ideally to make a dictionary.

Dictionaries have become a specialty of the English-speaking world. One reason may be the size of the vocabulary, because English has more words and more uses of words—more than two million in fact—than any other known language.

Americans, who make up the largest body of English users, appear to have a mania for linguistic correctness and a zeal for rectitude that has been built into the school system. We can thank (or blame) Noah Webster for much of this.

English developed from a standard English dialect established in the late fourteenth century; the English vocabulary expanded greatly in the sixteenth and seventeenth centuries. By the time of the eighteenth and nineteenth centuries, grammars and dictionaries had become essential.

Dictionaries probably began in the seventh century when monks made interlineal or marginal notes on manuscripts to explain hard words to their not-so-bright brethren. These were called glosses (hence, glossary). Not much happened lexicographically speaking from the seventh to the seventeenth centuries. In 1623 appeared the first book to be called *The English Dictionary,* a work by Henry Cockeram. He defined crocodile elaborately: "Having eaten the body of a man, it will weepe over at the head but in time eate the head also; thence the Proverb, He shed crocodile tears, viz. fayned teares."

This may illustrate why a new dictionary was necessary. In 1755 came Samuel Johnson's dictionary. Although a dramatic improvement over its predecessors, it had idiosyncratic definitions, as for example the word *lexicographer*—"a harmless drudge"; or *pension*—"pay given to a state hireling for treason to his country."

Although Johnson is popularly given credit as the great innovator in the field of lexicography, he owes much to his predecessor, Nathaniel Bailey, whose scholarly dictionary went through 10 editions, beginning in 1721. Johnson's contributions lay in editing. He brought to his work a sharp command of his native language, a mind stored with Latin and Greek classics, great energy, and disciplined judgment. He did more to bring order and good sense to our concept of English meaning than any other man who had come before him.

Although Webster only reluctantly admitted it, he owed much to Johnson. He derived his 1806 volume from *The New Spelling Dictionary* by John Entick, an English schoolmaster. This small work enjoyed wide circulation in America at that time. Entick, in turn, had derived his from Johnson.

Even Johnson had competitors. Dr. William Kenrick issued his dictionary in 1773, William Perry in 1775, Thomas Sheridan in 1780, and John Walker in 1791.

Three small American dictionaries had appeared before Webster's. Samuel Johnson, Jr., brought out the first in 1798, Caleb Alexander issued the second in 1800 to supplement his textbook business, and Johnson and John Elliott brought out a revised edition of the first in 1800. Webster approved "the general plan and execution" of the Johnson-Elliott work in a testimonial, although he misspelled Elliott's name. Yet none of these experienced much success because they proved little more than imitations and copies of earlier works.

Webster's five dictionaries, in order of their publication, are:

1. the *Compendious Dictionary* of 1806
2. two abridgements for school use that appeared in 1807 and 1817

3. the American Dictionary of 1828 (the greatest and most complete of the five)
4. abridgement of the 1828 issued in 1829 for family use
5. the "Counting House" Dictionary of 1841

Although the first of these dictionaries is derived from other works, it remains important for several reasons. First, in preparing it, Noah Webster learned and made use of the basic techniques of lexicography. If this endeavor had no other significance, that alone would be enough.

Secondly, the first dictionary began to create a market for dictionaries in America. It whetted the American appetite for this kind of reference work, an appetite that had been slight until this time.

Thirdly, although a flawed work, it was, in Samuel Johnson's simile, "like a flawed watch which is better than no watch at all." Despite its shortcomings, it posed a challenge to all competitors. It drove into oblivion the three earlier American works, as well as the English volume by John Entick. It surpassed them all in the five considerations that determine the success or failure of a dictionary.

The first of these considerations is the way a dictionary handles spelling. Although Webster retained in his first book some of the reforms that he had long advocated, he dropped the more radical ones. Many remained, however, to become the accepted orthography to this day. Perhaps Noah heeded the gentle and joshing criticism of his brother-in-law, Thomas Dawes, Jr., one of the few men who could make mild fun of Webster and get away with it. Dawes once wrote him: "But I aint quite ripe for your Orthography. Still, I dare not make up my judgment in a matter which has never been my study, against a learned, laborious, ingenious, experienced investigator."

The second of these considerations is the way a dictionary treats pronunciation. Webster wished to guard against capricious change and largely succeeded in his aim. Above all, he squelched the affectations of John Walker, which had won a large following in America, particularly around Boston. For example, Walker directed one to pronounce *a garden* as though it were spelled *egg-yarden* and *a guard* as though it were *eggyard*. This sent Webster into paroxysms of rage. But neither did all his pronunciations meet with success. He wanted to use *deef* for *deaf* and *ax* for *ask,* for example. Dawes dared twit him in this area, too: "Chooseday for Tuesday I cannot bear, and as to keind, it sits worse on my stomach than Indian Root."

The third consideration is the way a dictionary presents etymology. Many of Webster's theories about language proved wrong, eventually, but he hit the mark closer than did Johnson. The 1806 dictionary revealed to Noah that he still had much to learn in this area, so he set upon a self-study course that lasted more than 20 years. And he financed it entirely himself. There were no foundation or government grants in those days! Etymology and philology date only from the early 1800s as sciences. Evidently, Webster never did become familiar with the work and studies of Sir William Jones, a contemporary, who virtually founded the science of etymology. Nor can evidence be found that Webster made use of the efforts of two pioneering philologists who were also contemporaries, Jacob Grimm and Franz Bopp.

The fourth consideration is the degree of modernity of a dictionary. Webster's first dictionary contained the spoken and useful language of the time, including Americanisms, new words, and scientific terms.

The fifth consideration is, in many ways, the most important of all: how a dictionary handles definitions. Here Webster excelled. His attitude in defining a term was purely objective. He had the only true conception of a dictionary, that its function is to tell what words mean and not to pass judgment upon the ideas conveyed by the terms. He also had an impersonal attitude that forbade his giving expression, in his definitions, to his likes and dislikes. The only prejudice that could be found in the 1806 dictionary was his definition of a Federalist as "a friend to the Constitution of the United States." In later editions he eliminated even this mild bias because his political enemies had seized upon it.

The 1817 abridgement was similar to that of 1807, but it was reset in a larger format. Consequently it was the most successful of his dictionaries, and encouraged him to go on with his magnum opus, the 1828 edition.

As with all his books, Webster sought testimonials from many prominent and learned people—presidents of various colleges, elected officials, and well-known citizens.

Many educators lauded his work, especially at Yale and Princeton. Harvard faculty members, however, withheld praise.

John Quincy Adams, then teaching at Harvard, wrote a lengthy and learned reply, largely disagreeing with Webster's spelling reforms and quibbling about his pronunciations. Adams wryly acknowledged that his letter wasn't exactly what Noah had sought:

> Though not entirely coinciding with you in opinion upon these subjects, I hope you will be persuaded of the sincerity with which I appreciate your genius and learning, and of my respect for the depth and extent of your researches upon this and other subjects of high moment to our Country. I have thought a free and explicit avowal of my own impressions, would be most satisfactory to you in answer to the confidence with which you have favored me, although the principles which I have accustomed myself to apply in these cases have led me to deductions, differing in some respect from yours.

Despite Webster's frequent attacks on Thomas Jefferson, he asked the president to endorse the dictionary of 1806. There is no record that Jefferson did.

Although a slow starter with his early dictionaries, Webster enjoyed better timing than did Samuel Johnson. In 1755 English was a language of relatively minor importance in the world. By 1850, it had become a world language. Webster saw this coming. As early as 1824 he wrote: "The English Language will prevail over the whole of North America . . . it must within two centuries be spoken by 300 million of people on that continent."

Since 1850, it has spread all over the globe and is presently the international language. Even if there are more speakers of some varieties of Chinese than English, a fact not fully established, Chinese does not have the world authority, the geographic spread, the important literature, and the scientific writings, nor does it have the commercial significance of English. Although this eminence is not fundamentally because of the language's innate superiority, English is well fitted for its eminence and for the task of bringing various peoples together and establishing ties between them.

Webster saw some of these possibilities—however dimly. With the 1806 dictionary, he came to recognize that he had to do more than just criticize Samuel Johnson and the other giants of lexicography. He had to make his own, original dictionary. Thus began more than a score of years of persistent work "beating the track of the alphabet with sluggish resolution" (as Johnson saw the lexicographer's job).

Homer Babbidge summarizes Noah Webster's work thus: "Webster's burying himself in lexicography from about 1803 on is one of the most extraordinary stories of early America."

Chapter 16

STRIVING TOWARD THE GREAT DICTIONARY

Two personal tragedies tempered Webster's satisfaction—even delight—in having at last found a major goal in life.

A second son, Henry Bradford, born on November 20, 1806, survived for only nine weeks. Even before that tragedy had faded, another struck less than two years later. The Websters' youngest daughter, Louisa, was born April 12, 1808, mentally retarded.

Neither in his correspondence nor in his other writings does Webster, always reticent about his personal life, dwell on these double blows. But the testimony of his descendents, including that of his late great-granddaughter, Mrs. Howard B. Field, indicates that they troubled him deeply.

A tangible proof lies in Webster's religious awakening that also began in April 1808. Webster had been a freethinker on religion up until then, despite (or because of) his rigorous upbringing in the tenets of Calvinist Congregationalism. By the turn of the century he had even begun to lean toward Episcopalianism. He had gone so far as to suggest that his family join the Episcopal Church in New Haven. But his wife and daughters had been listening night after night to the revival sermons of the Reverend Moses Stuart, pastor of the Congregational Center Church. They urged Noah to reconsider. He did so with his customary intellectual vigor, augmented by his emotions at that time. The result was Webster's wholeheartedly embracing of Congregationalism to the extent that it became a dominant factor in his life for the rest of his days.

Characteristically, he wrote a careful statement of his new-found faith and beliefs and sent it to his brother-in-law, Thomas Dawes. Dr. Moses Stuart secured its publication in *The Panoplist,* and it soon became a pamphlet, *Peculiar Doctrines of the Gospel, Explained and Developed.* It enjoyed wide circulation and won praise from such dignitaries as the Reverend Abiel Holmes, father of Oliver Wendell Holmes: "I hope the publication of it will promote the interests of pure Christianity. . . . When men of learning and talents in *other* professions, voluntarily engage in the defense of our holy religion, the world is less apt to suppose them *interested,* and therefore more ready to listen to their arguments."

But little ever went easily for Noah. His newfound faith, or rather the pamphlet publicizing it, earned him still more enemies among members of other sects, but especially among Unitarians around Boston who thought it presumptuous of an "amateur" to lecture them about religion. This came at a particularly bad time for him because he was trying to raise money to finance his great project, a completely new dictionary.

Noah Webster had been trying to sell subscriptions in the Boston area for the proposed volume. *The Monthly Anthology,* a publication with Unitarian views, among whose founders was Ralph Waldo Emerson's father, began attacking the *Compendious Dictionary.* Moses Stuart wrote to Noah that "the *Anthology* is outrageous against you. . . . May the Lord turn their haughty and unfriendly designs into foolishness! Be assured, the object of their vengeance is more against your religion than against you."

Yet more than his religion harmed his sales efforts, as indicated in this 1809 letter written by the young Yale graduate Simeon Colton, then living in Salem, to his uncle, Simeon Baldwin:

Mr. Webster has just been in this town and in the neighboring towns soliciting patronage for his Dictionary to be published at some future day. . . . Mr. Webster seems determined to run down Johnson and build upon his ruin; nothing could be more fatal to him in this quarter, for our *literati* will never believe that he is superior to this great English lexicographer, and by this means will withhold the support they would grant were he more modest in his pretensions.

But there is another capital defect in Mr. Webster's proposition. He proposes that the subscribers should advance 10 dollars each. This I am certain will never succeed in this quarter, for their opinion of the man is not good enough to induce them, hardly, to become obligated to take his books after they are printed. . . .

Another thing which has been noticed is his peddling his own production in person; had he addressed the public thro the medium of the papers, or in handbills, with a specimen of his work, he would have been more successful. . . . But the great and capital defect is the unbounded vanity of the man. . . . I would not be censorious on the subject, for I wish the man success, but I wish he would be content to use the ordinary means to obtain it.

Webster never acknowledged or understood that such factors contributed to the failure of his campaign for subscriptions. At least, around Boston, he attributed his lack of success to religious prejudice.

Ironically, at about this same time Webster showed similar prejudice himself. He refused to endorse his friend Joel Barlow's epic poem, *The Columbiad,* because of its "atheistical principles." Their friendship ceased after Noah bluntly wrote: "No man on earth not allied to me by nature or by marriage had so large a share in my affections as Joel Barlow until you renounced the religion which you once preached and which I believe." This came after Barlow had agreed to subscribe to the dictionary.

Among the relatively few others who agreed to subscribe was John Jay. Furthermore, he paid his subscription. Some who had subscribed later reneged.

Failing in his subscription drive, Noah Webster turned to the government for possible help with a grant, or a job, or even a special commission, preferably abroad because he knew that he would eventually have to go to Europe to complete his studies. Rufus King wrote gloomily: "I am sorry to remark that I am able to discover but little probability of your receiving adequate encouragement to continue to devote your time and talents to the important and laborious investigation in which, for so many years, you have been engaged. Neither learning, morals, nor wisdom seem any longer to be regarded as objects of public esteem and favour."

Nor did Webster help his own cause in seeking government aid. In writing to President James Madison in 1809, he asked for assistance and then in the next paragraph lectured him on the evils of the Embargo and Nonimportation Acts. The lexicographer received no reply to either his request or his lecture.

On December 22, 1807, Congress had heeded President Jefferson's bidding and laid an embargo on all shipping in the ports of the United States. The purpose was to avoid being drawn into the Napoleonic Wars, since the combatants, especially Great Britain, were frequently stopping and seizing American flagships. L. W. Levy in his *Jefferson and Civil Liberties* comments:

From the beginning of the embargo throughout fifteen months of agonizing national trial, Jefferson's conduct impaired public liberty—and the success of his own policy as well. The embargo was the plan of an idealist, trapped and bewildered by the foreign situation, who gambled the nation's welfare on the outcome of an unrealistic scheme. He disdained criticism, brooked no opposition, and imperiously employed the most odious means to achieve his ends. The price mattered little. Constitutional principles, public understanding, sectional interest, national treasure—all were sacrificed for the policy to which he had overcommitted himself. Refusing to consider alternatives, he believed in that policy with a passion born of desperation and a dread of war. . . . In each respect Jefferson failed. The policy itself may have been admirable, but the manner of its adoption, execution, and defeat, for which he was responsible, was not.

To avoid foreign war, Thomas Jefferson made domestic war. He fought some of his own people, who believed that the national government had no right to deprive them of their ability to earn a livelihood.

Webster was among those whom the embargo caused great economic suffering. His book sales, especially of the speller, dropped alarmingly. But he opposed the embargo on broader philosophical and practical grounds. In a memorial to Jefferson protesting the embargo, he had written in 1808: "We know that an opinion has prevailed that a suppression of commerce will ultimately tend to encourage manufactures and render us less dependent on foreign commerce for articles of essential use. But in our apprehension this opinion is not well founded."

However, Webster deplored the violence of the reactions against the embargo, especially in New England, which had been hurt the most:

I hope the opposers of Mr. Jefferson's plans and measures will be tranquil, and leave the measures to have their natural effect upon the public. Passions are increased and opposition rendered more violent and fixed by a collision of opinions. The Federalists will do all they can to arrest the progress of bad measures, *in transitu,* but I think they had better be moderate in their opposition to them when passed. Such measures must in time work a cure. The evils we must suffer will be beyond calculation, but we had better submit to them than not to be cured.

The embargo failed to forestall the War of 1812. By the time it came, Webster had decided to move from New Haven to less expensive Amherst, Massachusetts. A letter of 1811 explains some of the circumstances:

I am engaged in a work which gives me great pleasure; & the tracing of language through more than twenty different dialects has opened a new & before unexplored field. I have within two years past, made discoveries which if ever published must interest the literati of all Europe, & render it necessary to revise all the lexicons, Hebrew, Greek & Latin, now used as Classical Books. But what can I do? My own resources are almost exhausted & in a few days I shall sell my house to get bread for my children. All the assurances of aid which I had received in Boston, N York &c have failed & I am soon to retire to a humble cottage in the country. To add to my perplexity the political measures pursuing render it almost impossible to sell property, or to obtain money upon the best security. A few thousand dollars, for which I can give security, would place me in a condition in the country to live with comfort, and pursue my studies—but even this cannot be obtained, till the measures of Congress assume a more auspicious aspect!

As usual with Webster, his plans took more time than he had anticipated to reach fruition. He actually did not sell his house until 1812 and did not move to Amherst until September of that year.

Why Amherst? Above all, living there was less costly compared to New Haven. It lay in the precinct of Hadley, near the colony that John Webster, Noah's ancestor, had helped found. Furthermore, friends and religious mentors recommended it as a place suitable to raise pretty daughters and a somewhat wayward son. Although only 11 years old, William was already showing signs of being unduly subject to the influence of rowdy city boys. His parents reasoned that a secluded country life would improve his behavior.

However, the older daughters joined the move under protest. Emily, the eldest, had reached an understanding with William Wolcott Ellsworth, the son of Chief Justice Oliver Ellsworth, under whom Webster had first studied law. Julia, the second daughter, wished to marry Chauncey A. Goodrich, a classmate of Ellsworth's in the Yale class of 1810. Just as the Websters were moving to Amherst, Goodrich had begun a Yale tutorship in New Haven.

Stifling their disappointment as best they could, the girls joined the five other children and their parents at Amherst. Webster had purchased a sizable house on the east end of Phenix Row (now the north or lower end of the Amherst Green). It was destroyed by fire in 1838, long after Webster had sold it and returned to New Haven. The property included 10 acres of land, and Noah was able to indulge his interest in horticulture. He raised all the family's vegetables and fruits, and established an orchard of apples, pears, peaches, and cherries that came to be the finest in town. He transplanted a grapevine from his father's farm in West Hartford whose sweet white grapes were new to the area.

Webster was no gentleman farmer, however. He was a serious agriculturist who experimented with fruits, potatoes, fertilizers, and many crops not common in Massachusetts, and who wrote about his efforts for *The Hampshire Gazette.* He also continued his 20-year campaign for forest conservation, warning of the dangers of deforestation. His voice truly sounded in the wilderness then because most Americans thought that trees should be cut down as rapidly as possible.

Noah loved farming and, in fact, believed that farming was "the first, best and most useful" occupation, and that property ownership remained the bulwark of a republican government.

The Websters brought new vigor to the village of 1,600 inhabitants and to the First Congregational Church. Webster and the three oldest girls organized a choir and actively participated in revival meetings. The Webster home became a social center for church affairs. In 1820 Webster organized a Sunday School. As usual, he found himself in controversies, even in church. He advised one minister to mend his ways. When he attempted to persuade the Second Congregational Church to merge with his First, he won only the ill will of many members of both.

Furthermore, he entered more serious disputes in politics. The war dragged on into 1814; business and commerce stagnated. Webster and others grew increasingly distressed at the inability of New England and other northern legislators in Congress to persuade the

Republicans (who were not to call themselves Democrats until
Jackson's time) to end the conflict. They saw this inability resulting
from abrogations of the Constitution, which had unfairly put governmental power in the hands of the Southerners. Northern legislators advocated certain Constitutional amendments to right what
they considered wrong, and urged legislatures in the Northern
states to vote for a Constitutional Convention.

Webster authored such a proposal, which was his platform in
running for and winning a seat in the Massachusetts legislature in
1814. The commonwealth's legislators voted for a Constitutional
Convention. A session was held in Hartford, Connecticut, in 1814,
attended by delegates from several states. Although the lexicographer was not a member, he played a conspicuous part in the organization of what became known as the Hartford Convention. The fact
that it met at all probably influenced the administration in Washington to begin peace negotiations. In later years many people, especially Southerners, thought the Hartford Convention had advocated secession. For the rest of his life Webster denied this and
explained that the convention intended only legitimate Constitutional reform. It represented his last serious fling in politics, and it,
too, was largely a failure. Although he was reelected to the legislature in 1815 and 1819, Noah remained a maverick. When his
charges of graft against the state printer were tabled (perhaps on
grounds of his bias against the trade), he quit Massachusetts politics
altogether. Writing to an acquaintance, he complained:

> The State of Massachusetts possesses a great deal of talent, enterprize,
> and wealth, and individuals distinguish themselves by many noble enter-
> prizes of great public utility. But, to be plain, Sir, I do not discover in this
> Commonwealth those comprehensive views of public interest and those
> prospective measures which tend gradually to augment the resources, the
> dignity, and prosperity of the State, which characterized the proceedings
> of some other States. . . . I have had so many intimations I am yet a stranger
> in the Commonwealth that I shall henceforth cease to concern myself with
> public affairs.

Some of these intimations had reached Webster in 1816 when
he had run for Congress. He had lost largely because his opponent
had charged that he was an outsider.

Webster never really liked public life. What he loved was the private world of the farmer or lexicographer. He found relief in both, but especially in the study of language. When he had seen the *Compendious Dictionary* off the presses, he began to complete the unabridged dictionary that he had started as early as 1800.

At first Webster had set modest goals—to correct errors that earlier compilers had missed and to add new scientific and other words that had entered the language. As he studied the words, however, he found that their etymology was almost virgin territory. The discovery excited his scholarly instincts. He turned aside after finishing the first two letters of the alphabet to prepare a synopsis of the connections between the 20 languages he had learned.

For 10 years Webster labored on *A Synopsis of Words in Twenty Languages.* He never published this lengthy work because of its expense, the difficulty of obtaining the necessary type, and the fact that it had no market. Yet he incorporated some of his preliminary findings into *A Philosophical and Practical Grammar of the English Language,* which he issued in 1807 in an attempt to revive his grammar for children. It missed its market because it was too erudite. The *Synopsis,* too, was immensely learned—a storehouse of philological lore, as a result of his effort to bring together words whose form might throw light on the affinities of languages and on the primary sense of each word. Work on the *Synopsis* gave him the basic tools for defining accurately the root meaning of each word.

While in Amherst, surrounded by his large family, Webster worked methodically on the *Synopsis.* In his upstairs study, overlooking hills on which now stand buildings of Amherst College, he had a semicircular table two feet wide, on which he put his reference books. Starting at the right end of the table, he would go through his grammars and dictionaries while tracing a particular word through 20 languages, all the time writing notes on his discoveries. He sat in a chair mounted on casters so that he could move from one end of the table to the other more easily.

At four o'clock, Mrs. Webster brought him fruit or nuts and cake, a signal for him to remove his spectacles and relax. Perhaps one or more of his children would visit with him, although the older daughters were by then beginning to leave home.

On September 14, 1813, William Wolcott Ellsworth married Emily and took her to Hartford, where she joined in his political successes as congressman, governor, and Supreme Court justice.

On May 22, 1816, Harriet married Edward H. Cobb, son of a wealthy West India merchant in Portsmouth, New Hampshire. Julia soon afterward, on October 1, 1816, married Chauncey Goodrich, who within a year accepted the professorship of rhetoric at Yale, a post he held for the next 40 years.

In 1818 Mary, Noah's favorite, married the widower Horatio Southgate of Portland, Maine. Her death in childbirth only a year later cast a shadow over her father for the rest of his life. The baby, also named Mary, survived. The Websters adopted her, and she helped ease the sorrow of her mother's loss.

Harriet, in the meantime, lost both a child and husband, and returned to the Amherst home. William Webster blundered from one school and occupation to another, disingenuously confessing to "a native imbecility of mind." Yet Noah always forgave him "because he is my only son, and you know I love him." William's sisters loved him, too, but he also exasperated them. They never quite had the courage to voice fully that exasperation to their father. Only Mary had ever quite dared to stand up to him, and she had died.

Webster ruled his family by the Old Testament code. Yet he showered affection and concern on all. He proved to be the classically indulgent grandfather to all his children's children, although their grandmother smoothed the path with backstage promptings on how best to deal with their formidable grandfather. Most of the grandchildren paid frequent and lengthy visits, and when they had returned home, he wrote them all letters, some in Latin, and insisted on return mail. He was lenient, however, about their spelling and grammar.

All during his Amherst period, Webster continued his annual sales trips, but now he combined them with visits to his married daughters. The sons-in-law suffered his visits largely in silence.

It would seem that Webster's family affairs, lexicography, farming, miscellaneous writings, sales trips, and local and state political work would keep two men busy. Somehow, while engaged in so many other activities, he mustered the time and energy to found Amherst College.

Amherst Academy began in December 1814 as a secondary school. Webster was "the master spirit" in that institution, which educated all his younger children, including William. Opposition in the community delayed its charter until 1815, but Webster resolved that difficulty. He served as vice president of the academy's board of trustees from 1816 to 1820. On August 10, 1820, he became president, and 13 months later the college formally opened with 47 students. Webster had been campaigning for the college for four years previously, but money shortages delayed its opening. It was billed as a "charity institution in Amherst for pious young men." Its original goal was to educate them for the ministry. The Amherst trustees had vainly tried to persuade Williams College, in the northwest corner of Massachusetts, to move to Amherst. Webster led that forlorn effort. Undaunted, he then turned to raising funds for a new institution. In laying the cornerstone for the South College, he repeated his creed of education:

> The object of this institution . . . is to second the efforts of the apostles themselves, in extending and establishing the Redeemer's empire—the empire of truth. It is to aid in the important work of raising the human race from ignorance and debasement; to enlighten their minds; to exalt their character; and to teach them the way to happiness and to glory. Too long have men been engaged in the barbarous works of multiplying the miseries of human life. Too long have their exertions and resources been devoted to war and plunder; to the destruction of lives and property; to the ravage of cities; to the unnatural, the monstrous employment of enslaving and degrading their own species. Blessed be *our* lot! We live to see a new era in the history of man—an era when reason and religion begin to resume their sway, and to impress the heavenly truth, that the appropriate business of men, is to imitate the Savior; to serve their God; and bless their fellow men.

With the establishment of the college in 1821, Webster resigned his post as president because his lexicographic work had fallen behind schedule. At 63 years of age he feared he might not have enough time left to finish his great work. Even so, he had accomplished more than most men could ever dream of accomplishing; he had contributed to virtually every aspect of education; he had taught school, written textbooks, founded secondary schools, and now founded a college.

To complete the dictionary, Noah Webster needed to be close to a fine library. His family had become smaller because of his daughters' marriages. Thus, his household expenses had dropped. The nation's economy had improved and so had the sales of his books, especially of the speller. Webster could afford to return to New Haven. In 1822 he did just that.

Chapter 17

THE GREAT DICTIONARY IS BORN

Noah and Rebecca Webster returned to New Haven with joy. Their somewhat shrunken family consisted of the widowed Harriet Webster Cobb, the orphaned Mary Southgate, and Eliza, William, and Louisa.

The Websters settled temporarily for a year in a rented house at the corner of Wall and College streets while they awaited the construction of much larger quarters nearby at the corner of Temple and Grove streets. Yale's Silliman College now includes its site. The house was dismantled in 1938 and moved to Henry Ford's Greenfield Village in Dearborn, Michigan, where it still stands. While dismantling the house, workmen discovered that Webster's study on the second floor had double walls. The lexicographer needed quiet.

The house was carefully built in the Federal style, designed and constructed by David Hoadley, a well-known architect of that time. An elliptical louvered window and modillion cornice are typical of Hoadley's interpretation of the Classical Revival style.

The Webster family watched the progress of this building with much fond anticipation. Eliza wrote: "A glad one was the day we moved into more commodious quarters. . . . We sat on low chairs and sewed the parlor carpet ourselves." At Christmas the family decorated the fluted Ionic columns on the classic entrance porch with evergreen roping. Sprigs of holly, Christmas wreaths, and a candle-laden tree cheerily accented the handsome house during the Christmas season.

The Websters continued their competent and gracious hospitality. New Haven neighbors often praised their musicales, charade parties, and frolics. Noah Webster still enjoyed parties, just as he had in his youth and early manhood.

Webster followed his disciplined routine of writing and working on the dictionary every day until 4:00 P.M. He worked at a secretary because he no longer needed the semicircular table now that he had stopped work on the Synopsis.

Both Noah and his wife were proud of their children. In a letter to a married daughter, Mrs. Webster wrote: "Papa longs to see you all. I heard someone conversing in the drawing room the other day and found him standing before your portraits. . . . We often talk together . . . of our singular happiness in our sons-in-law and daughters and such a promising bunch of grandchildren."

Rebecca, too, could look on the brighter side of things and try to forget the retardation of one daughter, the death of another, and the prolonged adolescence of her only surviving son. At one point, she wrote of him to Noah: "Poor William! I wish he had more decision of character, what will become of him?" William never succeeded at much of anything except playing the flute. He completed studies at neither Yale nor Middlebury colleges. While at Amherst Academy he had embarrassed himself and his family as the result of a drinking episode. He worked in a store in Hartford for a while, but his employer sent home poor reports on him. In 1824 at the age of 23, he remained at loose ends. His father decided to take him to Europe while he finished the dictionary. The degree of Noah Webster's desperation about William can be measured by the fact that he could barely afford to finance his own trip, let alone his son's.

By 1820 Noah had already spent nearly $25,000 of his own money and $1,000 of his subscribers' funds on his lexicographic labors. After financing the construction of his new house and supporting his family, he had nothing left for his long-planned visit to European libraries. Fortunately, the widowed Harriet Webster Cobb came to the rescue and lent him $1,000.

While meticulous in his financial dealings with people other than his relatives, Webster had different standards when it came to business affairs with family members. No evidence exists that he ever repaid fully the loan from his father for his education, the sums

that brother-in-law James Greenleaf advanced him at the start of his
marriage, nor the loan from Harriet. Perhaps the lenders never
seriously expected to be repaid. In a sense, Noah did repay some
of his family debts, but informally. In his father's old age, Webster
frequently sent him small sums, as he did also to other relatives.
Upon his and Rebecca's deaths, more of the family possessions
were willed to Harriet's family than to the other children, probably
because of the unrepaid loan.

Webster tended to spare no expense in his large projects but
to be niggardly in small matters. For example, in those days when
the recipient of mail paid the postage, he chided his correspondents
for writing on heavy paper or for not writing on both sides of the
sheet. Many of these complaints came while he visited the libraries
of Paris, Cambridge, and London. Although he was too busy to
write many letters, he wanted mail from his family.

Young William's diaries provide much of the information
about the father's and son's European sojourn that began in June
1824 and ended in June 1825.

"Blessed with sea-sickness," notes William in an entry for June
17, 1824. The principal entertainments aboard ship were whist,
dominoes, chess, and cockfighting. Noah Webster detested the
latter, as he did all blood sports.

While on board ship, Noah gave a short address to observe
July 4, "dwelling chiefly on the advantages that have actually ac-
crued to both England and France since the separation of America
from the old country." His toast for the occasion: "Our families and
the friends we love."

Father and son had bad quarters in Le Havre. Everywhere,
William found French prices, living conditions, food, customs, and
morals unfavorable when compared to their American counter-
parts. At Rouen, seven porters seized their luggage and demanded
35 francs for 10 minutes' work. Noah gave them eight and then had
to call the maitre d'hôtel to get rid of them.

In Paris, the pair found rooms at Madame Riviere's, No. 19
Rue Bergere, for 180 francs each per month plus tips. The elder
Webster happily went to work in the Bibliothèque du Roi with its
800,000 books and 80,000 manuscripts.

William Webster's Calvinism (perhaps reflecting his father's
views) shows in a comment about the Royal Palace in Paris: "De-

spite the fascinating gloss thrown over it, the glance of an experienced man will perceive this palace is the abode of corruption and every species of vice."

Samuel G. Goodrich, an acquaintance, encountered the lexicographer in Paris and wrote: "I saw a tall slender form, with a black coat, black small-clothes, black silk stockings, moving back and forth, with its hands behind it, and evidently in a state of meditation. It was a curious, quaint, Connecticut-looking apparition, strangely in contrast to the prevailing forms and aspects in this gay metropolis. I said to myself—'If it were possible, I should say that was Noah Webster!' I went up to him, and found it was indeed he. At the age of sixty-six, he had come to Europe to perfect his dictionary!"

Although Webster delighted in the library's facilities, he didn't grow enthusiastic about much else in France. He remarked of Versailles: "You would be delighted to ramble in the gardens of the palace. . . . But I perceive all the kinds of plants or nearly all are to be found in the large gardens in New York and Philadelphia." He commented on the Parisian (and most other) theater: "Before I can believe the stage to be a school of virtue, I must demand proof that a single profligate has ever been reformed or a single man or woman made Christian by its influence." Perhaps shocked by the style of life he found in Paris, he wrote Rebecca, "Man has but little time to spare for the gratification of the senses & I would therefore caution you against the fascination of plays, novels, romances."

His wife had some advice for him, too: "I fear you suffer people to take you in, & don't keep a good lookout. But I suppose the French cheat with so much politeness & civility that you have no disposition to complain."

He did admire the Parisian ladies, but from a discreet distance. All his life Webster retained his eye for feminine beauty, and he always enjoyed the company of women more than the company of men.

Webster arose every morning in Paris at six, worked two or three hours before breakfast at 9:30, then went to the library, returning to his rooms in time for dinner at 5:00 P.M. He liked the two-meals-a-day routine, but he never enjoyed French food. The elder Webster spent his evenings with his son William, either helping him with his French studies or accompanying him on sight-seeing trips or other forms of recreation, which often meant strolls, for Noah remained an indefatigable walker.

He originally planned to stay in Paris for only one month, but his studies required three. Even so, he had to forgo work with one reference source at the library because the institution closed during the month of September. Father and son left Paris on September 13, 1824, heading for Cambridge University in England. Webster would have preferred Oxford, but no one at that university had ever answered his letters of request. Nor did anyone at either institution respond favorably to his proposals for standardized English in both spelling and pronunciation.

Furthermore, English customs inspectors made things difficult for the Americans. Finally they got through the bureaucratic problems and headed for Cambridge, via London. Webster had made arrangements through Samuel Lee, professor of Arabic at Cambridge, to spend the winter at the university and use the university's library of 100,000 volumes.

He and William found lodgings with a Mrs. Emmerson at Downing Terrace, a series of semidetached, graystone houses, some of which still stand. The name derives from its proximity to Downing College, then in the process of being established.

Webster described his quarters in a letter dated September 24, 1824, to his wife: "I am now settled very snugly at lodgings for the winter. I have three rooms, a parlor & two bed rooms. The parlor, where I now sit & where William & I write & take our meals is about 14 or 15 feet square. In this we have two little cabinets, two tables, a sofa & a few chairs, a handsome glass over the fire place, where we have a coal fire. Back of this is my bed room, about ten feet square, where I have a good bed, a bureau, looking glass &c. William has a small bed room in the Chamber, my rooms are on the lower floor. . . . We board as well as lodge in the family, & Ann, the old servant, is very obliging. The expense is not greater than in Paris."

On September 22, William noted more pessimistically in his diary: "My father is almost discouraged. . . . The morals of a greater part of the population are wretched and depraved. . . . If the servant can find no opportunity to pilfer & cheat, the mistress will. This filching disposition is increased continually by the carelessness of the gownsmen of the university who have no regard to expense, &

to whom it is a matter of indifference whether they throw away their money or whether it is stolen."

Although the Cambridge dons received the Websters with reserve (partly because Professor Lee fell ill and could not introduce them widely), work on the dictionary went well. Noah wrote to Rececca:

I have enjoyed very good health in Europe, & at no time for forty years past, have I been able to accomplish more business daily, than I have both in France & England. My indispositions, from which I am rarely free, are slight & do not interrupt my studies. I have great cause of gratitude. ... I shall finish the copy of my dictionary, all but revising it, by the month of May—perhaps sooner. As this work can not be printed at present in the United States, for want of type, I shall send a petition to Congress to grant me the privilege of importing copies of the book into the United States, free of duty, for five years, till the character and success of the work shall be ascertained.

Webster miscalculated again on the timing; he finished it sooner than expected. He described the completion of his great work thus:

"I finished writing my Dictionary in January 1825 at my lodgings in Cambridge, England. When I had come to the last word, I was seized with a trembling which made it somewhat difficult to hold my pen steady for writing. The cause seems to have been the thought that I might not then live to finish the work, or the thought that I was so near the end of my labors. But I summoned strength to finish the last word, and then walking about the room a few minutes, I recovered."

Well might a man in his 67th year tremble from exhaustion after more than a quarter century of study and research and the laborious preparation *alone and by hand* of almost 70,000 word definitions. That was 12,000 more than had appeared 70 years earlier in the work by Johnson and a staff of assistants. Webster was the last major lexicographer in English to work alone. The task of making a dictionary now requires a team of experts.

Webster was wrong in still another expectation—that he would get the dictionary published in England. In February 1825 he left Cambridge for London to revise his work, study further at the British Museum, and to find a printer.

So confident was he that he had already enlisted Daniel Webster's assistance to push through a special act of Congress to import the work into the United States duty free. To his dismay, no English publisher would accept it, even though the American ambassador, Richard Rush, had tried to help. The publishers in London had similar or related projects already in hand and refused to take on something that would compete with them.

Yet Webster quickly recovered from his disappointment, booked passage home, landing in New York on June 18, and returned to New Haven on the next day. He received a hero's welcome from family, friends, and Yale faculty members. Honors came to him thick and fast. Phi Beta Kappa had elected him a member on November 11, 1824 while he was studying in Cambridge. The prestigious Bunker Hill Monument Association had made him a member on March 16, 1825. Earlier, Yale had awarded him a doctor of laws degree in 1822. Ironically, he had traveled far and wide to receive the recognition that he was now receiving at home.

For a while, Noah Webster feared he would have to finance the publication of the dictionary himself. For six months he sought backing. Finally, Sherman Converse agreed to take on the job, although Webster had to endorse a large note to seal the deal. Converse then obtained the necessary type from Germany.

Webster issued an advertising prospectus on March 3; it was far more temperate than the broadsides he had written for earlier publications. Partly because of that and partly because the public at last recognized, however dimly, that Webster had produced something monumental, there was a generally favorable reaction to his announcement. Although he criticized rival dictionaries, as usual, Webster contented himself with factual claims about the advantages of his work, which included primarily words in common use, provided verb participles—a new departure for dictionaries—noted terms occurring frequently in historical works, and gave legal, technological, and scientific terms. He modestly pointed to his definitions, noting that "the defining part of a dictionary is by far the most important."

To help him in the burdensome task of reading proof and checking details, Webster hired his new son-in-law William Fowler, who had married the widowed Harriet on July 26, 1825. Also, he took on Denison Olmsted, later a Yale professor, to check scientific terms, and James Gates Percival, an eccentric poet, who proved more hindrance than help. Percival had studied Bopp, Grimm, and the other new German philologists. He challenged many of Webster's etymologies, and cautioned that the work should be delayed until all derivations could be conclusively tracked down. Webster overrode his objections because, at 69, he thought the work might never get published during his lifetime if he met all of Percival's objections.

He adopted, perhaps unknowingly, Johnson's dictum that a faulty dictionary is better than no dictionary at all. Percival later attacked the dictionary's imperfections, especially in etymologies. That component is probably the weakest in the work simply because time ran out on Webster.

But the other four components necessary in any dictionary—spelling, pronunciation, illustration, and definition—have stood the test of time. Webster dropped many of the more extreme orthographic experiments that he had insisted upon as late as 1817. Such spelling reforms that he kept—*jail* for *gaol, center* for *centre, labor* for *labour,* etc.—remain to this day in American usage. He modified his New England pronunciations to some degree, but the pronunciation common in America today is, by and large, the pronunciation favored by New Englanders in the early nineteenth century, as interpreted by Webster. The illustrations he used were homely and commonsensical. He broke completely with the previous lexicographic practice of culling nearly all illustrations from literature. In definitions, of course, he was superb.

The definitions give this edition its lasting quality. Webster believed that "there is a primary sense of every word, from which all others have proceeded; and whenever this can be discovered, this sense should stand first in order." He came to this conclusion as a result of his work on the *Synopsis.* Here he surpassed Johnson, who had haphazardly listed synonyms and definitions. In addition, Webster meticulously discriminated between the various meanings of a word. For example, he explained the shadings in the senses of the word *clever* in English and American usage this way:

Clever In New England, good-natured, possessing an agreeable mind or disposition. In Great Britain, this word is applied to the body or the intellect, in respect to adroitness of action; in America, it is applied chiefly to the temper or disposition. In Great Britain, a clever man is a man of a pleasing, obliging disposition, and amiable manners, but often implying a moderate share of talents.

Besides preparing good definitions, Webster added many new words, both technical and nontechnical. Examples of the nontechnical words used occasionally then and commonly now include *accompaniment, advisory, editorial, appreciate,* and *demoralize.* This last is the only word he actually coined.

Hezekiah Howe began printing the work on May 8, 1827, in New Haven. The last pages came off the press in November 1828. The bulky format required 2,000 pages in all, 1,000 in each of two volumes, and sold at 20 dollars per set. Webster braved the bad weather to deliver in person the first two completed sets to his old friend and benefactor, John Jay, in Westchester County, New York.

The dictionary met with widespread critical approval, although a few die-hard Bostonians didn't like it and some Britishers scorned it, but on thinly veiled nationalistic grounds. James Madison atoned for previous digs at Webster by praising his "learned research, elaborate discrimination, and taste for careful definition."

Congress adopted his dictionary as the standard in its halls, and various American courts made it standard. Many foreign governments declared it their official dictionary for English.

Astonishingly, the work sold best in England. More than half of the original 2,500-copy American pressrun went to Britain. Webster granted E. H. Barker, an English scholar, permission to bring out an English edition. This appeared in parts between 1830 and 1832, with 3,000 copies of the set being sold. Thus, an American scholar established the standards for the English language, even in England.

And except for the German-cast type, it was totally an American enterprise. With pride, Webster titled it *An American Dictionary of the English Language.* His preface bristled with such nationalistic statements as "our country has produced some of the best models of composition . . . equalled only by that of the best British authors, and surpassed by that of no English compositions of a similar kind." Despite these remarks, it sold better in England than in the United States.

The problem in America arose from the fact that Webster couldn't supply the demand. As a result of speculations unrelated to the dictionary, Sherman Converse, the publisher, went bankrupt and the dictionary became tied up in litigations that stemmed from his bankruptcy. In the meantime, other American and English dictionaries appeared, some of them little more than superficial reworkings of Webster's 1828 edition.

Webster's most serious competition came from Joseph E. Worcester, whom he had commissioned to prepare an abridgement of the great dictionary in 1829. In 1835 Worcester pieced together a much larger work under his own name that enjoyed some success.

Before Converse's bankruptcy, Noah had earned barely enough from the American edition to pay his editorial assistants. To protect his interests, Webster had to bring out a new edition. In 1838, at the age of 80, he mortgaged his home to finance it. Because of the unusually long time needed to print and proofread the work, it didn't come out until 1841, when he was 83 years old.

Noah may not have been unduly anxious to get the new edition to market until then because all the 1828 volumes, freed at last from impoundment in the Converse bankruptcy case, had not been sold by 1840.

The 1841 edition was even larger than that of 1828. It, too, developed only a modest market. All of Webster's dictionaries probably never returned him an income that matched the sums he had paid out of his own pocket during his years of lexicographic labors. The venerable speller continued as his main source of financial support. From time to time, other books, such as *The Prompter*, and various textbooks, helped him financially for limited periods of time. One example is *Letters to a Young Gentleman*, issued in book form in 1823. The letters are avuncular in tone and offer a touch of Lord Chesterfield, without his advice on sex. The volume enjoyed good sales for a while. The *Letters* indicate the marked versatility of Webster's writing style. He could be earthy, humorous, vigorous, learned, sarcastic, eloquent, or passionate as the occasion demanded.

Chapter 18

SPELLING BOOKS AND BIBLES

When the 70-year-old Webster finally brought out his masterpiece, *An American Dictionary,* in 1828, he deserved a rest. Instead, he faced a new crisis. His speller, upon which his financial well-being depended, was meeting unprecedented competition and attacks that threatened its sales. The septuagenarian countered the challenge with the vigor of a man half his age.

In the labor and distraction of completing the dictionary, the lexicographer had neglected the speller. He had not altered it since 1804. In the meantime, Webster had spelled many words in a new way in the *Compendious Dictionary,* but had kept his speller's orthography in his *School Dictionary.* Some spellings were slightly different once again in *An American Dictionary.* He had let the orthography in the speller alone, fearing that changes would harm the sale or encourage competition. As a result, he waited almost too long to update the speller. By 1827 a competitor finally sensed the sales value of a campaign based on the lexicographer's inconsistencies. At this time, Webster's speller and books derived from works by the Englishman Walker shared the lucrative speller field. Bostonians especially favored the Walker approach to spelling and pronunciation. Three new spellers, each based on Walker, came out in 1825 in upstate New York. Each denounced Webster and lauded Walker.

Their arrival alarmed Webster for nationalistic as well as economic reasons. He feared that his long fight for an American style of pronunciation and spelling, which he had thought won, would receive a setback. To attempt to dampen the increasing reverence for the Walkerian approach to language, Webster wrote this in 1826:

As I was an ardent republican in principle (in 1783) and had exposed myself as a volunteer to the hardships of the field in defense of my country, I felt a peculiar pride and a degree of enthusiasm in contributing my feeble efforts to detach my country from an undue dependence on our mother country for our opinions and books. . . . I desired to see my countrymen disposed to give a due preference to all their native productions, to promote all efforts to exalt the literary character of their country, and to disengage themselves from thraldom of an overweening reverence for foreign opinions and authority—*a species of slavery that hangs like a millstone about the neck of all literary enterprize in the United States.*

He wrote to son-in-law William Fowler that "the utterance of many Walkerisms operates on me like a box on the ears." What particularly irritated him was that the new competitors plagiarized his format and teaching methods used in the speller, while denouncing him and urging Walkerian pronunciations.

"I have examined some of the books which are sent into the world to correct the evil I have done," he wrote. "One of them [by Elihu H. Marshall] is little less than a copy of mine—it contains almost all my tables, with no alteration except the transposition of a few words. No less than sixty or seventy pages of it are wholly mine. . . ."

Although Marshall plagiarized the most, only Lyman Cobb, the author of one of the other three newcomers, responded. And he did so vigorously, pointing out—in newspaper articles, in talks to teachers, and to anyone else who would listen to or read him— all of Webster's inconsistencies. He also found many prominent educators and others to endorse his work. In short, he copied the master, Webster, in sales techniques.

Lyman Cobb copied the master in still another way. He pointed to the need for a new broom, making the telling point that Noah's speller had been around for more than 40 years and had not been revised since 1804—precisely the kind of argument the young schoolmaster used decades before in successfully supplanting Dilworth.

Noah counterattacked on two fronts. First, he employed Daniel Barnes, a New York schoolmaster, to edit *The American Spelling Book* so that it would conform to the great dictionary. Unfortunately, Barnes died in an accident before he could finish the job. Webster gave it to another New Yorker, Aaron Ely, who completed the task for 1,000 dollars.

Immediately the detractors claimed that the new *Elementary Spelling Book* was Ely's more than it was Webster's. Noah replied: "It is a palpable falsehood I will not notice." He was right because Ely's work consisted chiefly of rearranging and reclassifying some of the elements and finishing the task of bringing the orthography into conformity with the great dictionary. If anyone could share the credit with Webster, it was Cobb who had pointed out many of the shortcomings that were later corrected.

On the second front, the lexicographer renewed his personal selling efforts, spending two months a year on the road. He scored still another coup by getting many new endorsements for the revised speller. While in Washington successfully getting the nation's copyright laws reformed, he won from more than 100 members of the judiciary and of both Houses of Congress signatures endorsing many of his books, from the great dictionary to the speller. He published these and many others in a small pamphlet which he distributed all over the United States.

Although Cobb did not surrender, he had to fight a long retreat, and Webster's book ultimately won the war. Noah still fought skirmishes on the plagiarism front, but his speller and dictionary continued as the standard for American spelling during the rest of his life and until the end of the century.

Beginning in 1830, the septuagenarian author prepared seven more schoolbooks. Two were related to the speller. The first appeared in 1831 as *The Elementary Primer,* a 36-page paperbound, extensively illustrated pamphlet. Webster had long resisted the use of so many pictures as a hindrance to thorough learning, but he succumbed with this one for children. It proved highly successful and contained the popular poem, "Twinkle, Twinkle, Little Star." The second schoolbook, published in 1833, redid his old spelling book, issued because many printers continued to print it despite his objections. He added new passages, most of them sententious.

In *The Teacher; a Supplement to the Elementary Spelling Book,* Webster in 1836 organized thousands of words under their respective subject headings and gave simple definitions.

Among the seven new texts were three reading books. *Biography, for the Use of Schools* (1830) offered 37 brief biographies of people from Homer to William Cowper, the eighteenth-century English poet. Twenty-one Americans appeared in it, including Noah's ancestor Governor John Webster. In 1836 came *The Little Franklin: Teaching Children to read what they daily speak, and to learn what they ought to know.* In words of one and two syllables it offered lessons and truths useful in life. It actually was *The Prompter* rewritten for children. The third reader was an attempt to reissue the old Part II of the *Institute,* the reader, which had long been out of print. In 1835 the canny author simply dressed it up.

The seventh—and most important—of the books was the *History of the United States,* a book that became widely used. Although Webster had been the first author to include American history in schoolbooks, he did not issue a text with this title until 1832. He was the first to honor the Puritans as the founders of one of the first genuine republics in the New World:

For the progress and enjoyment of civil and religious liberty, in modern times, the world is more indebted to the Puritans in Great Britain and America, than to any other body of men, or to any other cause. They were not without their failings and errors. Emerging from the darkeness of despotism, they did not at once see the full light of Christian liberty; their notions of civil and religious rights were narrow and confined, and their principles and behavior were too rigid. These were the errors of the age. . . .

The Puritans who planted the first colonies in New England, established institutions on republic principles. They admitted no superiority in ecclesiastical orders, but formed churches on the plan of the independence of each church. They distributed the land among all persons, in free hold, by which every man, lord of his own soil, enjoyed independence of opinion and of rights. They founded governments on the principle that the people are the sources of power; the representatives being elected annually, and of course responsible to their constituents. And especially they made early provision for schools for diffusing knowledge among all their members of their communities, that the people might learn their rights and their duties. Their liberal and wise institutions, which were then novelties in the world, have been the foundation of our republican governments.

The role of the Puritans is now widely acknowledged by American historians, but Webster was the first to point it out.

While the schoolbook projects enjoyed success and merited

respect, Webster launched another with more dubious results. He appointed himself a committee of one to translate the Bible.

Since the publication of the great King James Version, many other translations had appeared, some by only one man. These include a version by W. Mace, printed in 1729, and celebrated for its vulgarity, another by Antony Purver, printed in 1764, with amendments to support the doctrines of the Quakers. Dr. Alexander Geddes produced a version for English Catholics in 1792–97. There were many other versions produced for other sects. So, Webster had considerable precedent. But he did not have the resources to turn out a great Bible. Substantial as his scholarship was in Hebrew, Greek, and Latin, or fervent as his religious zeal was, he had too many religious prejudices, too little religious scholarship, and too little time. He produced a corrected, sterilized, and bowdlerized version of the King James.

In preparing his version of the King James Bible, Webster made three types of alterations. First, he corrected grammatical errors. He thought this had to be done or such mistakes would creep into everyday speech. A few examples suffice. The King James Version of 1611 translates Matthew 16:13 as "whom do men say that I, the son of man, am?" Webster changed it to "Who do men say that I the Son of man am?" He straightened out tenses and regularized *shall* and *will* and *should* and *would.* He clarified the reference, "strain at a gnat, and swallow a camel" to "strain out a gnat." So far so good.

Webster began running into trouble with his second type of alteration, the substitution of contemporary for obsolete words. Here he lost some of the style and color that have given the King James Version so much of its beauty. He disliked *gather together* and substituted *assemble, collect,* or *convene.* For *three score* he wrote the prosaic *sixty.* He discarded *gave up the ghost* and chose *expire* instead. *Peradventure* yielded to *perhaps, laugh to scorn* to *deride, safe and sound* to *in health.*

Webster became ridiculous in his third type of change. He substituted euphemisms and other expressions for "language which cannot be uttered in company without a violation of decorum or the results of good breading." For *breast,* he substituted *bosom,* for *leg, limb.* He deleted or used euphemisms in every Biblical reference to a bodily function involving elimination or sex.

Noah Webster's revision of the Bible failed, not because it was bold, but because it was trivial. It contributed little to Biblical literature or study.

Yet, it was a major publishing venture. It appeared in October 1833. By taking no royalties, Webster kept the retail price at two dollars. Even so, the Bible enjoyed only modest sales. Many preachers and religious writers objected to his translation. As late as April 6, 1835, he wrote: "I do not know that any person has yet hazarded a commendation of the work. I stand alone and unsupported, even by gentlemen who agree with me in the importance of the revision. In this, as in some other efforts of mine at real improvements, I am either not supported, or opposed by men who claim to be the directors of public instruction." Later in the same year he continued his complaints: "I wish a few clergymen would summon courage to commend my Bible to the public. It wounds my feelings to observe how indifferent the public are, and especially clergymen, to the correction of faults in the common version." Taking a hint, the Yale faculty issued a cautious approval. That helped, at least in Connecticut and in the Congregational Church.

Demand was sufficient to justify a less expensive edition of the New Testament only in 1839. His entire Bible was reissued in stereotyped form in 1841. In 1833–34 he wrote a companion for his edition of the Bible, a work of 180 pages entitled, *Value of the Bible, and Excellence of the Christian Religion: For the Use of Families and Schools.* The handbook sets forth the nature, contents, and value of the Bible. In it Webster states his religious credo, which also explains why he embarked on the overambitious translation project:

We must be careful to distinguish the real religion taught by Christ and his apostles, from those systems which interested men have established. We find the true religion of Christ in the Bible only. It is a scheme wonderfully simple, the principles of which are all comprehended in two short phrases, *love to God* and *love to men.* Supreme love to God, the source and model of all excellence, is the foundation of the whole system of Christianity; and from this principle in the heart flow all the benevolent affections and exercises which constitute practical piety. The persons who love God supremely will reverence His character and laws, and will extend his benevolent affections and charities to all his creatures. From this source will proceed love to man, and the careful performance of all moral and social duties.

Noah Webster considered the translation of the Bible his crowning achievement, because it completed his philological studies and because it rounded out his plan to give to the United States a body of basic literature framed in correct language. While he was wrong that the translation was his best work, he had noble motives in attempting it. And he was not the first author to misjudge his own works. His edition of the Bible had largely vanished by the late nineteenth century.

Translating the Bible, writing and selling textbooks, and preparing new editions of his dictionary didn't take all Webster's time during the 1830s. He kept an eye on political events, and what he saw didn't often look good to him.

Although now regarded as a prophet in New Haven, he seldom was looked on in this fashion elsewhere. The presidency of Andrew Jackson from 1829 to 1837 especially disturbed him. He saw Jackson as merely a lesser Jefferson and therefore almost as bad.

In a letter to a daughter, Mrs. Webster described what was probably a familiar Websterian scene: "Your Papa is sitting in his rocking chair with a paper in his hand, and a large pile before him. Once in a while a deep groan escapes from him at the critical state of our country."

Noah frequently criticized Jackson's policies in public. On December 27, 1832, he wrote: "All heads are puzzled and all hearts solicitious for the fate of our Constitution and public peace." He recaptured some of his old polemical fire in writing on April 17, 1834: "We are indeed in a singular condition. President Jackson has his foot upon our necks and a great portion of the people of New England justify him. What is our republicanism worth?" He still had little confidence in the ability of people without property to rule, and wrote to Daniel Webster on February 9, 1835: "I see by the proceedings of Congress that measures are taken to destroy the independence of the judiciary and to give the people a full swing in other things. Thus we shall be able to give a full trial of a republican government to the people of the United States. On this gloomy subject I must forbear comment."

Nor did he have confidence in youthful voters. He once proposed that the voting franchise be limited to those 45 and older.

While he was out of step on these matters, Webster showed an amazing prescience elsewhere, demonstrating once again his fundamental ability as a political scientist. In another letter to Daniel Webster written in 1837, when he expressed alarm at the growth of the spoils system under Jackson, he observed:

There is a great defect in the Constitution of the United States which if permitted to exist, will ultimately shake the government to its center. This defect is, the want of some effectual provision to prevent candidates from seeking the office of chief magistrate by corrupt and illegal means. So long as the president has the bestowment of most of the offices, and the power of removal from office at pleasure, the most daring and unprincipled intrigue for the office has the best chance for success. . . . These avenues must be closed.

The office of President is a prize of too much magnitude not to excite perpetual dissensions; and if the contentions for the office of chief magistrate do not ultimately overthrow our constitution, it will be a miracle.

After Martin Van Buren succeeded Jackson, Webster felt keen disappointment when it grew clear to him that the new president would carry on with the Jacksonian philosophies. In August 1837, his old newspaper, now called the *New York Commercial Advertiser and Spectator,* carried an article by him under the pseudonym, Sidney, that said in part:

It has been a prevailing opinion, even with many of our greatest men, that the *people* can govern themselves, and that a *democracy* is of course a *free government.* Such language as this has been in the mouths of our patriots, and in the columns of newspapers, for thirty or forty years, until it is considered as expressing political axioms of unquestionable truth. The men who have preached these doctrines have never defined what they mean by the *people,* or what they mean by *democracy,* nor how the *people* are to govern themselves, and how *democracy* is to carry on the functions of government. But in practice the word *people* denotes any collection of individuals, either in meetings legally assembled, or in mobs, collected suddenly, no matter how, for any purpose good or bad.

Our writers have uniformly charged the tyranny of civil government to *Kings,* and true it is that Kings have often been tyrants. But it seems never to have occurred to such writers that the people, so called, are just as bad as Kings. By nature, all men have the same passions as Kings—they are all selfish—all ambitious—*all,* from the King or President down to the corporal of a militia company, aspiring to power. . . . The whole sin of the old Washington federalists consisted in attempting to incorporate into our government, or establish by law, some power which should effectually control or prevent popular violance. . . . And it is a melancholy truth that fills us with alarm, that the people will not create a power which shall effectually defend their own personal rights and safety.

The Sidney article enraged the Democratic press, especially because other newspapers reprinted it, and it was reissued in pamphlet form as *Voice of Wisdom.*

The Democrats kept trotting the Sidney article out for the next four years as evidence of what the reactionaries would do to the new Democratic forces. Webster never publicly acknowledged his authorship, probably because it grew increasingly clear that it had done more harm than good to his dwindling band of Federalists who would soon give up that name altogether to regroup with other conservatives to call themselves Whigs.

Webster took a more conservative view on slavery, too, an issue that was agitating the nation more and more as the 1830s advanced. The man who had helped found an early abolitionist society in Hartford before the turn of the century now advocated a gradual approach to emancipation. In effect, he said "a plague on both your houses" to the New England abolitionists and to the advocates of slavery. In an 1837 letter to his son William, he wrote: "The Abolitionists are infatuated and their opposers worse. I see no end to our disorders."

The next year, he wrote again to his son: "Abolition too is taking a high tone in New England, & the anti-slavery society in Hartford, I am told, have demanded of the candidates for our Senate a *pledge* that they will favor the cause. This is a degree of effrontery which was hardly to be expected in Connecticut. I look on our public affairs with alarm."

In his 80th year, Noah at last had the wisdom not to go to the public with such views. He had mellowed—a little. In New Haven, his fellow citizens regarded him with pride as a patriarch. Elsewhere in the nation some of his unpopular political viewpoints were being forgotten or overlooked. Noah Webster was known now as the great American maker of dictionaries.

Chapter 19

"LOOK IT UP IN WEBSTER"

With the great dictionary published, Webster felt he had at last reached his goal. Although he continued busy for the rest of his days, gone was the peripatetic quality of his early activities. He had arrived.

Many visitors now came through the Webster door on Temple Street in New Haven—some without knocking. Yale professors called regularly, as did old-time Federalists, neighbors, clergymen, and the merely curious. The lexicographer sat usually in a high-backed arm chair on one side of the fire in the front sitting room, his wife in a rocking chair on the other, receiving one and all.

Among the curious was Anne Royall, a feminist author and traveler, who reported: "In a few minutes, a low chubby man with a haughty air stepped into the room; his face was round and red and by no means literary looking. He was dressed in black broadcloth, in dandy style; in short, he comes nearer the description of a London cockney than any character I can think of. He eyed me with ineffable scorn and scarcely deigned to speak at all. I am sorry for his sake I ever saw the man, as it gave me infinite pain to rescind an opinion I had long entertained of him."

Mrs. Royall must have aroused Webster's prejudices against assertive, unfeminine women because he was normally voluble in female company. Furthermore, no one else ever described him as "low" with a "round" face. He had a lantern jaw and was close to six feet in height and slender until his old age. He did favor an old-fashioned style of dress, usually black, and he had the ruddy complexion of a redhead.

When Noah was 80, his favorite granddaughter, Emily Fowler (then 12 years old), described him: "Tall, erect and slender, but not thin in face and figure. As a young man he had brown eyes, sometimes called gray, and abundant hair, well cared for, of an auburn tint, and the fair ruddy skin that accompanies reddish hair."

In his eighties, his hair was thinner than in his younger days, when he had difficulty managing it—a fact seldom hinted at in his various portraits. He never grew bald, but he was gray by 85. He retained a quick, swift, light step, often called "elastic" by contemporaries, and had shapely hands, feet and legs—perhaps the reason he continued to wear breeches and silk stockings long after they went out of style.

The octogenarian remained a temperate and dainty feeder, although he retained the sweet tooth that he had had all his life. For breakfast, he normally had coffee, a slight relish (usually some spiced meat), and a piece of toast. For dinner at noon, he enjoyed meat, a vegetable, fruit, tea, and a glass of Madeira. His supper consisted of a "dish of tea," bread, butter, and sweetmeats. He liked preserves and jams and always had raisins and a bag of peppermints in his study that he shared liberally with his grandchildren.

He spent every morning in his study and took an afternoon walk, often accompanied by a visiting grandchild. He visited the post office twice a day because he carried on a voluminous personal and business correspondence. His calligraphy stayed legible right up to his death, although it had lost the flowing quality of earlier years. Even into the 1840s he still sometimes used the long "s" and ampersand favored in the eighteenth century.

In private Noah Webster was usually laconic or taciturn, but in company he could grow animated if the subject or visitors interested him. His temper, which he long ago had learned to control, occasionally showed when visitors uttered an indelicate remark in his presence. Emily Fowler said his "refinement of nature and innate modesty were feminine." Nobody ever reported hearing him swear or even use expletives. He had a Quaker-like purity of mind that matched his straitlaced appearance. He once considered expurgating Shakespeare and other great English writers in a revised edition like his version of the Bible. Fortunately, he dropped the idea.

Webster hated vulgarity and obscenity so much that such language aroused flaming rebuke if he heard it from his children or grandchildren. A grandson reported that he "shivered like a top" after a dressing-down from his grandfather for bad language.

Many of Webster's family members, but especially his children, chafed under his patriarchal rule. The eldest daughter, Emily Webster Ellsworth, complained to her sister Harriet, "We are treated like boys and girls." They hoped he would yield responsibility for some of his business affairs to them, but he never did during his lifetime. He gave some business to the hapless William, but this was a make-work project because his son blundered from one misadventure to another and needed financial support.

William had married Rosalie Stuart of Fairfax, Virginia, a descendent of Martha Washington. He could never support Rosalie to her satisfaction, and the couple eventually separated. Their two sons died without issue as a result of wounds and illness suffered during the Civil War, one having fought for the North and the other the South. Thus, Noah Webster had no direct descendents bearing the Webster name after the deaths of his grandsons.

But the marriages of the other Webster children prospered. Eliza Webster, the sixth child and fifth daughter, married Henry Jones in 1825. They founded a school in Bridgeport, Connecticut. With Mary Webster Southgate's death, Eliza became her father's confidante because she backed him in his projects, even when he mortgaged the Temple Street house to bring out the new edition of the dictionary in 1841.

The patriarch had attempted to get financial support for the new edition from his sons-in-law, but none had given it. He felt particularly aggrieved that William Ellsworth, Emily's husband, and William Fowler, Harriet's spouse, had refused. Ellsworth had long kept his distance from his father-in-law, and so had Fowler, a brusque, somewhat pompous man. Fowler, an Amherst professor, thought he should have become the editor of the dictionary upon Noah's death, but the quiet Chauncey Goodrich, Julia's husband and a Yale professor, received the assignment. Goodrich had earlier joined Webster in various publishing ventures.

The old axiom that opposites attract worked in the case of Noah and Becca Webster. While he was tall, she was short. While he dealt mostly with outside, public matters, she loved the everyday affairs of homemaking. He was usually somber, she usually gay and effervescent.

To Harriet she wrote in 1833: "Your Papa . . . bids me say

that his Bible is progressing. I must go now and read what Louisa calls a pious proofsheet, which will close the prophet Isaiah. So you see, dear Pod, after helping your father make his Dictionary, I am still assisting him in his literary pursuits. You doubtless remember the fable of the fly on the coach."

She had a streak of iron in her, however. Her daughters complained of her "tenacity of superintending rule." As she grew older, she wrote frequently that she felt "feeble," but in the next line she would recount her domestic exploits.

The family's conditions of health loomed large in all the domestic correspondence. Here are some examples from Noah's letters to various relatives:

My health is good, though I get slight catarrhal affections when I go abroad.

Emily is, I think, in rather better health than when she arrived.

I caught a cold in riding from Quincy to Boston last Monday, but it is becoming mild & I trust will not prove troublesome.

[Julia] is now convalescing, & we trust free from danger.

Your mother is better than when she left home. Your sister Harriet has a bad cough—and all her children have the hooping cough.

Emily has not entirely recovered from illness caused by an injury to a tendon in the knee. Harriet is better & Eliza has recovered from a severe attack of quinsy.

Webster himself often suffered from severe eyestrain because of much reading. He was also subject to cricks in his back, sciatica, and nightmares. To avoid disturbing his wife, he usually slept on a narrow bed in his study.

In October 1839, Noah and Rebecca, aged 81 and 73, observed their golden wedding anniversary. For unknown reasons, but probably because of difficulties in getting all the family together, the celebration didn't occur until May 1842. By this time a missed deadline bothered no members of the family, and they enjoyed a typical Websterian celebration, as described by Eliza Webster Jones:

All the children, grand-children, and great grand-children of the dear, dear old Patriarch and his wife Rebecca were invited to gather at brother Goodrich's on Wednesday, the 4th of May. Through the favor of a kind Providence, we came together in health and comfort at the appointed time, and sent a troup of happy little ones to escort the head of our house to the gathering table. Brother's parlor was filled. 35 of us were there, and only one absent [probably Harriet because of illness]. Sister G. took her seat by Father's chair on the carpet and I, mine on the other side. Pretty soon the six little boys came and seated themselves like Turks before him, and a little wee thing of 3 years left her picture books and came and squatted down so innocently at the end of the row that all were greatly amuzed. There were only two present who could not sing, and all began in merry mood good 'Auld Lang Syne' and then 'Home, Sweet Home' and tears of tenderness and joy followed. We dined at ½ past one in the back parlor, the table being arranged on three sides of the room, and father and mother in the middle and the daughters on the one side, sons-in-law on the other and the grandchildren arranged in families, and my only brother, his wife and the great grand babies opposite the patriarch. Oh, it was a pleasant sight! When all were seated at the well filled board, brother G. rose and fervently implored the blessing of heaven. We felt that God was with us and it was a cheerful meal. When we had finished brother Fowler made a few remarks expressive of our gratitude to God that we had been permitted to meet in such comfort, and that we were so united, loving and beloved, and returned solemn hearty thanks. Then we returned to the parlor to talk of old times. . . . At five we all went to Father's and took our tea in the home of our early days. In the evening before we parted, our beloved and revered parent called our attention, and kneeling, as we all did, fervently implored the blessing of heaven upon us, our children and our children's children to the latest generation. Oh shall not that prayer be heard. Then rising, he said, it was the happiest day of his life, to see us all together; so many walking in the truth and the others, children of promise. Oh, E. I cannot tell you half he said. Then he presented each of us with a Bible, his last gift.

In 1842, he put together miscellaneous essays and wrote new ones for *A Collection of Papers on Political, Literary and Moral Subjects,* a 373-page volume that went to press in April 1843. It proved to be the last book he published during his lifetime, although he finished correcting a new edition of the speller in May.

"My literary labors are now completed," he said, a statement he had uttered several times before.

On May 22, 1843, Webster wrote what probably was the last letter he ever penned to his son William. Typically, it dealt with business, asking William about plans for a selling trip to the West and inquiring about suspected instances of pirating in Cleveland.

On Sunday, May 21, 1843, he attended church all day. It was warm and he wore lighter clothing than previously. On Monday he walked to the post office twice, as usual, but noticed that he had a chill. He had contracted pleurisy and at first seemed in no danger. His condition, however, had worsened by Friday. He died quietly on Sunday, May 28.

Funeral services were held at the Center Church in New Haven and at Amherst College. Noah Webster is buried just around the corner from his home in the Grove Street Cemetery in New Haven, with his wife who died four years later following a stroke, and other family members.

In his will he gave to his wife all household effects and $750 per year for her and Louisa to live on. He gave $300 annually to Louisa to live on if she survived her mother. One thousand dollars went to each of three daughters, Emily, Harriet, and Eliza. To Julia and Chauncey Goodrich, went 37 cents in royalties on the sale of each copy of his great dictionary for 28 years. He gave other property to other daughters and to his adopted daughter, grand-daughter Mary Southgate who had married Henry Trowbridge, Jr., in 1838. Son William received his books and papers.

Although Noah Webster died in 1843, his name remains alive today as a synonym for dictionary—"look it up in Webster." But he also lives through his ideas on copyright, the United States Constitution and, above all, his contributions toward unifying and standardizing the American version of the English language through his dictionaries. He literally helped invent America. His dictionary, of course, continues to this day, having outsold through its various editions every book in the English language except the Bible.

The dictionary, after his death, seemed to take on a life of its own. In 1843, G. & C. Merriam Company of Springfield, Massachusetts bought the publishing rights and unsold copies of the 1841 edition for $3,000 in a kind of distress sale. The unsold sheets had been stored by the printer, J.S. & C. Adams, in Amherst. Although the Merriams had dealt with Webster before, the relationship between the two parties had not been uniformly cordial because the company had once inadvertently pirated his speller. They had made amends, and Webster was on as good terms with Merriam as he probably could be with any printer or publisher. The posthumous match that was made was the beginning of a long relationship between Merriam and the Webster heirs.

Merriam employed the Webster son-in-law, Chauncey A. Goodrich, to edit an enlarged and improved edition of the dictionary. He completely revised it, and a one-volume edition appeared in 1847 at six dollars. It sold so well that when the copyright was renewed Merriam was able to pay the Webster family $250,000.

An 1859 edition introduced illustrations for the first time. In 1864, the 1847 edition was superseded by *Webster's Unabridged,* edited by Noah Porter, who eventually became president of Yale. Merriam began to have piracy trouble after the copyright had expired and the 1847 edition had been withdrawn. This led in 1917 to a court ruling that required rival publishers who used the Webster name to print a disclaimer in their books and advertising, saying, "This dictionary is not published by the original publishers of Webster's dictionary or their successors."

The next complete revision came in 1890, again under the direction of Porter. This became a truly international dictionary and the standard for the 300-million member English-speaking world.

In 1900, an extensive supplement of new words appeared. The next revision, *Webster's New International Dictionary,* came out in 1909. By 1934 rapid expansion in all fields of knowledge required Merriam to remake the dictionary as *Webster's New International Dictionary, Second Edition.* The Third Edition appeared in 1961. Merriam puts out other and smaller versions, including the popular Collegiate. Also, other publishers issue reference works with the name Webster in the title. Altogether, Webster's name appears in more than 50 entries in *Books in Print.*

English speakers employ dictionaries to an extent greater than users of any other language. Reasons for this include the tongue's enormous vocabulary and the amorphous nature of its spelling. Another reason may be habit, begun by the half forgotton Dictionary War in the late nineteenth century.

Webster inadvertently laid the groundwork for this so-called war. It arose from the publication in England in 1853 of Worcester's *Universal and Critical Dictionary of the English Language,* which included this statement on the title page: "Compiled from the

Materials of Noah Webster, LL.D., by Joseph E. Worcester." In the American edition Worcester had claimed in his preface that he had used nothing of Webster's work, but this claim did not appear in the English version's preface.

Merriam published a pamphlet, *A Gross Literary Fraud Detected,* that dealt bluntly with Worcester. Worcester's publisher replied. It charged that Merriam was simply trying to blow up Webster's reputation when in actuality Noah "was a vain, weak, plodding Yankee, ambitious to be an American Johnson, without one substantial qualification for the undertaking, and the American public has ignored his pretensions!"

A pamphlet war began, both publishers probably realizing that the publicity helped sales of both dictionaries. Yet the dispute went beyond a mere publicity gimmick. Librarians and academicians began testifying of their own volition about the relative merits of the rival works. Newspaper articles on the subject appeared, sometimes matching in length and heat the mounting controversy at this time about slavery. In the meantime, the man on the street began buying the dictionaries in increasing numbers to judge for himself.

The publicity man's dream lasted until about 1864 when the *Webster's Unabridged* became unquestionably the best English dictionary in the world.

The 1864 edition still rested on the 1828 unabridged. Noah Webster had started it all. Van Wyck Brooks in his *The Flowering of New England* comments: "He [Webster] did his task so well, within his limits, adding his thousands of words, adding his tens of thousands of definitions, which no previous book had ever contained, that 'Webster,' with its countless modifications, was destined to remain the standard work for the English-speaking people of the world."

Babbidge in his collection of Webster's nationalistic prose says this about the great dictionary:

Thus did Noah Webster perform single-handedly a symbolic act of independence for America and fulfill in part his vision of America as a nation eminent in arts as in arms. The impact of this single work upon American culture may well have exceeded the aggregate effect of Noah Webster's direct appeals for a heightened sense of cultural independence. In many respects, the preface to Noah Webster's monumental dictionary represents matured nationalistic views. Absent are the radical enthusiasms of youth and the acid overtones of his irascible disillusionment. The almost secure tone of this composition reflects Webster's recognition of the essential validity of his position and the ultimate worth of his lexicographic efforts. The obvious pride with which he cites evidence of an emerging American literature suggests [he] felt at least a part of his vision of America had been achieved.

Thomas Pyles in *Words and Ways of American English* summarizes: "In many respects this Yankee schoolmaster is a far more appropriate symbol of our young nation than is either the cosmopolite printer-philosopher Franklin or the squirish-minded Washington."

Bibliography And Sources

GENERAL SOURCES

Previous biographies of Noah Webster:

Ford, Emily Ellsworth Fowler, *Notes on the Life of Noah Webster*. Emily Ellsworth Ford Skeel, ed. 2 vols., original edition privately printed, 1912; reprinted 1971 by Burt Franklin, New York.

Fowler, William Chauncey. *A Dictionary of the English Language*. New York, 1846. A sketch of Webster's life is included.

Goodrich, Chauncey A. *An American Dictionary of the English Language*. New York, 1847. A sketch of Webster's life is included. This is expanded in *The American Literary Magazine*, Jan., 1848.

Scudder, Horace E. *Noah Webster*. American Men of Letters series, Boston, 1881.

Warfel, Harry R. *Noah Webster, Schoolmaster to America*. New York, 1936. Reprinted New York, 1966.

Books that deal with aspects of Webster's life, works, or times:

Babbidge, Homer D., Jr., ed. *Noah Webster: On Being American*. New York, 1967.

Bowen, Catherine D. *Miracle at Philadelphia*. Boston, 1966.

Hansen, Allen O. *Liberalism and American Education in the Eighteenth Century*. New York, 1926.

Leavitt, Robert Keith. *Noah's Ark, New England Yankees and the Endless Quest*. Springfield, Mass., 1947.

Levy, Leonard W. *Jefferson and Civil Liberties*. Cambridge, Mass., 1963.

Peterson, M.D. *Thomas Jefferson and the New Nation*. New York, 1970.

Shoemaker, E.C. *Noah Webster: Pioneer of Learning.* New York, 1936.

Sloane, Eric. *Diary of an Early American Boy, Noah Blake, 1805.* New York, 1963.

Warfel, Harry R., ed. *Letters of Noah Webster.* New York, 1953.

Woodress, James. *A Yankee's Odyssey–The Life of Joel Barlow.* Westport, Conn., 1969.

Webster and members of his family wrote thousands of letters. The major repositories of unpublished letters include the libraries of Amherst College and Yale University and the New York Public Library's Gordon L. Ford Collection. A score of other libraries in the United States and England also have some of his letters.

OTHER SOURCES.

Chapter 1.

Connecticut Courant, 1764–74.

Historical Society of West Hartford.

Tunis, Edwin. *Colonial Living.* New York, 1957.

Chapter 2.

Baldwin, Ebenezer. *Annals of Yale College.*

Connecticut Antiquarian, June, 1954.

Dexter, Franklin Bowditch. *Sketch of the History of Yale University.*

Dwight, Timothy (the elder). *Columbia: A Song,* written and set to music by Dwight; printed at the Press of Timothy Dwight College, Yale University, New Haven, 1942.

Etude, Jan., 1938.

Chapter 3.

Connecticut Courant, June 1, 1781.

Johnson, Samuel. *The Rambler,* 1750–52.

Benton, Joel. "An Unpublished Chapter in Noah Webster's Life, Love and the Spelling Book." *Magazine of American History,* July 1883.

National Portrait Gallery of Distinguished Americans. Vol. II, New York, 1834–39.

Paine, Thomas. "Letter to the People of France." In *Complete Writings.* Philip S. Foner, ed. New York, 1945.

Chapter 4.

Dilworth, Thomas. *New Guide to the English Tongue.* London, 1740.

Earle, Alice Morse. *Child Life in Colonial Days.* New York, 1899.

Lester, Rev. Charles Edwards. *Glances at the Metropolis.* New York, 1854.

Magazine of American History, Dec., 1830.

The Quill, May 1964.

Saturday Review, October 18, 1958.

Sloane, Eric. *Museum of American Tools.* New York, 1963.

Warthin, Dr. Alfred Scott. "Noah Webster as Epidemiologist." *The Journal of the American Medical Association,* March 17, 1923.

Chapter 5.

Publishers Weekly, October 20, 1958.

Chapter 6.

Hobbies, October 1958.

Chapter 7.

American Mercury, August 16, 1790.

Bibliographic Society of America, 1938.

Connecticut Courant, 1783, 1785.

Chapter 8.

Blum, John M. et al. *The National Experience.* New York, 1963.

Dictionary of American Biography.

Hamilton, Alexander. *The Continentalist, Complete Works.* H.C. Lodge, New York, 1904.

Chapter 9.

The Essex Journal, September 13, 1786.

Yankee, April, 1966.

Chapter 10.

Freeman, Thomas. *The Freeman's Journal,* April 17, 1787.
PTA Magazine, May, 1965.

Chapter 11.

Duyckinck, Everet A., editor, *Cyclopedia of American Literature,* 1875.

Chapter 12.

Appleton's Cyclopedia of American Biography.
The Quill, May, 1964.

Chapter 13.

Bookman, January, 1933.
Journalism Quarterly, September, 1934.
Vidal, Gore. *Burr.* New York, 1973.

Chapter 14.

The Literary Digest, February 28, 1920.
Warthin, Dr. Alfred Scott. "Noah Webster as Epidemiologist." *The Journal of the American Medical Association,* March 17, 1923.

Chapter 15.

American Heritage Dictionary of the English Language, Introduction, New York, 1970.
Dictionary of American Biography.
Gore, Philip B. Introduction to *Webster's Third New International Dictionary.* Springfield, Mass., 1961.
Life, February 12, 1958.
School and Society, November 3, 1945.

Chapter 16.

Fuess, Claude Moore. *Amherst, the Story of a New England College.* Boston, 1935.
Hitchcock, Frederick H. *The Handbook of Amherst, Massachusetts.* Amherst, Mass., 1891.
Thompson, Everett E. "Noah Webster and Amherst College." *Amherst Graduates' Quarterly,* August, 1933.
Tuckerman, Frederick. *Amherst Academy, A New England School of the Past: 1814–1861.* Amherst, Mass., 1929.

Tyler, W.S. *History of Amherst College During Its First Half Century.* Springfield, Mass., 1873.

Chapter 17.

Bryan, J. "The United States' Least-Known, Best-Known Man." *The Saturday Review,* April 11, 1942.
Kingsley, J.L. Review of the 1828 dictionary in *North American Review,* March, 1830.
Wagenknecht, Edward. *Virginia Quarterly Review,* April, 1929.
Yankee, April, 1966.

Chapter 18.

Cobb, Lyman. *A Critical Review of Noah Webster's Spelling-Book.* Albany, 1828.
Cobb, Lyman. *A Critical Review of the Orthography of Dr. Webster's Series of Books for Systematick Instruction in the English Language.* New York, 1831.
Condit, Blackford. *The History of the English Bible.* New York, 1896.
Mencken, H.L. *The American Language.* New York, 1923.
Warfel, Harry R. "Centenary of Noah Webster's Bible." *The New England Quarterly,* September, 1934.

Chapter 19.

Brooks, Van Wyck. *The Flowering of New England.* New York, 1936.
Greenfield Village. New York, 1972.
Mercantile Library Reporter, 1855.
Pyles, Thomas. *Words and Ways of American English.* New York, 1963.
Royall, Anne. *Sketches of History, Life, and Manners in the United States.* New Haven, 1826.

Index